A CONCISE HISTORY OF WESTERN PHILOSOPHY

ALSO AVAILABLE FROM BLOOMSBURY:

Why Cicero Matters by Vittorio Bufacchi
Epictetus's 'Encheiridion' by Scott Aikin and William O. Stephens
Philosophers on Consciousness by Jack Symes
Plato and Nietzsche by Mark Anderson

A CONCISE HISTORY OF WESTERN PHILOSOPHY

From Platonism to Nihilism

MARK ANDERSON

BLOOMSBURY ACADEMIC
LONDON • NEW YORK • OXFORD • NEW DELHI • SYDNEY

BLOOMSBURY ACADEMIC
Bloomsbury Publishing Plc
50 Bedford Square, London, WC1B 3DP, UK
1359 Broadway, New York, NY 10018, USA
29 Earlsfort Terrace, Dublin 2, Ireland

BLOOMSBURY, BLOOMSBURY ACADEMIC and the Diana logo are trademarks of Bloomsbury Publishing Plc

First published in Great Britain 2025

Copyright © Mark Anderson 2025

Mark Anderson has asserted his right under the Copyright, Designs and Patents Act, 1988, to be identified as Author of this work.

Cover design by Louise Dugdale
Cover image: Collapsed columns around the Temple of Zeus in Ancient Olympia in the Peloponnese of Greece.
Richard Garvey-Williams / Alamy Stock Photo

All rights reserved. No part of this publication may be: i) reproduced or transmitted in any form, electronic or mechanical, including photocopying, recording or by means of any information storage or retrieval system without prior permission in writing from the publishers; or ii) used or reproduced in any way for the training, development or operation of artificial intelligence (AI) technologies, including generative AI technologies. The rights holders expressly reserve this publication from the text and data mining exception as per Article 4(3) of the Digital Single Market Directive (EU)

Bloomsbury Publishing Plc does not have any control over, or responsibility for, any third-party websites referred to or in this book. All internet addresses given in this book were correct at the time of going to press. The author and publisher regret any inconvenience caused if addresses have changed or sites have ceased to exist, but can accept no responsibility for any such changes.

A catalogue record for this book is available from the British Library.

A catalog record for this book is available from the Library of Congress.

ISBN: HB: 978-1-3505-5598-3
PB: 978-1-3505-5599-0
ePDF: 978-1-3505-5600-3
eBook: 978-1-3505-5597-6

Typeset by Deanta Global Publishing Services, Chennai, India

For product safety related questions contact productsafety@bloomsbury.com.

To find out more about our authors and books visit www.bloomsbury.com and sign up for our newsletters.

For Mike, Ronnie, and Ginger,
my teachers.

Special thanks to my wife, Francesca, for her support and encouragement. My thanks also to Scott Aikin, Troy Anderson, M.C. Cunningham, Andy Davis, Brandon Frazer, Paul Loeb, Ben Smith, and Bloomsbury's anonymous readers, all of whom provided valuable comments on various chapters of this book.

Plop Top and Ned Z wander the ways wondering side by side. Through ever a day never a night undelighted with spiraling gripes as years wheel round kaleidoscopic, inside and out around.

Plop, says Ned, for instance, there's nothing here, nothing with us, that's not been with us here before, and behind before.

I see, Plop Top replies, but if something never dies, then surely nothing ever abides in no place at no time. But look around: Nothing's nowhere, no?

Yes, true, I suppose that's so, if somewhere truth there be; but if everywhere there be none, as we're both aware that none there be—well, now, doubtless you agree.

We, say you? Not so! Not me!

—Hmph! —Hmm... Nor I, may be.

He toes the stones then ha ho! both and nook-in-crook they go—on dusty roads past verdant tumuli—strolling, struggling, lollygaggling, gesticulating, sophisticalizing, stretching and skipping hilariously, even to this day, this very today indeed. Now, then, and everywhen, for fun and all for free.

—A fragment from the notebooks of Michael Tommasi

CONTENTS

Preface: Being versus *Becoming* ix

1 One and Many 1
2 Parmenides 5
3 Heraclitus 9
4 Gorgias 13
5 One and Many 19
6 Plato: Ontology 23
7 Plato: Epistemology 29
8 Plato: Objectivism and Relativism 35
9 One and Many 41
10 Aristotle: Ontology 45
11 Aristotle: Ethics 51
12 Plotinus 59
13 Sextus Empiricus 65
14 Augustine 71
15 Thomas Aquinas 79
16 William of Ockham 89
17 Descartes 95
18 Hume 101
19 Kant 107
20 Nietzsche: Platonism Inverted 113

21 Nietzsche: Metaphysical Nihilism 119
22 Nietzsche: Psychological Nihilism 125
23 Being and Becoming 133

Suggestions for Further Reading 141

PREFACE

BEING *VERSUS* BECOMING

This little book is organized around the theme of *Being and Becoming*, which terms function in philosophy as shorthand for two opposed worldviews. Each encapsulates in a word many ideas that by their complex associations constitute a network of interwoven concepts and contentions. "Being" suggests immateriality, eternity, order, the really real, and the objective knowledge of truth, goodness, and beauty. "Becoming" evokes corporeality, ephemerality, change, the perspectival, and the subjectivity or relativism of all cognition. Plato is the premier philosopher of Being, Nietzsche the peerless advocate of the philosophy of Becoming.[1]

In the *Republic*, Plato writes of the realm of Being, and more specifically of that which stands at its pinnacle, that it's the source of all intellectual, ontological, moral, and aesthetic value, in both the personal and the social-political spheres:

> The Idea of the Good . . . is the cause of all that is upright and beautiful in all things, generating in the visible realm both light and the source of light, and in the intelligible realm it itself is the source producing truth and understanding . . . and anyone who

---

[1] I set aside for now their great predecessors, Parmenides and Heraclitus. And as to my designating Plato "the premiere philosopher of Being," I don't mean to suggest that Becoming plays no role whatever in his account of reality. It does, but it's inferior to Being in every way.

would act prudently either in private or in public must behold this Good. (*Republic* 517c)

In his early essay *On the Advantage and Disadvantage of History for Life*, Nietzsche remarks that the modern privileging of Becoming over Being must lead, at least among the masses, to the degeneration of traditional practices of personal and political virtue:

> If . . . the doctrines of sovereign Becoming, of the fluidity of all concepts, types, and kinds, of the lack of any cardinal difference between man and animal—doctrines which I take to be true but deadly—are flung at the people for one more lifetime in the current mania for education, then let no one be surprised if that people perishes of pettiness and misery, of ossification and selfishness, that is, if to begin with it disintegrates and ceases to be a people. (Hackett, 1980)

The peoples of the ancient and medieval West lived under the reign of Being. Intellectually, this manifested in the preeminence of one form or another of Platonism (even Christianity was saturated with Platonism). Belief in Being gradually declined in the era spanning the late-medieval and early-modern periods; it fell further, and faster, during the later phases of the scientific revolution and then the Enlightenment; and by the nineteenth century the advent of Becoming was at hand. Nietzsche announced its arrival at the tail-end of the century, and he identified nihilism as its dark companion; but no one much listened to him. By the middle of the twentieth century, however, he could no longer be ignored: the world, and our understanding of the world, were unmistakably in flux. Today there's more or less general agreement, if not in theory at least in practice: Being is indeed a fiction; God is dead; and nothing remains but the ceaselessly shifting currents of the river of Becoming, nihilism riding on the waves.

What follows is a concise account of the intellectual history of the West in its transition from a Platonic affection for Being to a Nietzschean bacchanal of Becoming.

1

One and Many

The senses reveal a world of many individuals, but the mind is drawn to the notion of an underlying unity. As the polytheist pantheon appears upon reflection to be a manifestation of a single divinity, so the manifold teeming before our eyes can seem but the dream of a solitary consciousness. The primordial metaphysic of the Indo-Europeans: the apparent Many is really One.

The Hindu Brahman is the archetype: the unchanging, ever-abiding, unmanifest root of earth and sky and all things in between. The Vedic Trimurti—Brahma, the creator of the universe; Vishnu, its sustainer; and Shiva, who destroys it—and the infinite array of gods and men and all things else over which they reign are merged within their profoundest depths as the singular Reality of Brahman. The apparent Many is really One.

The so-called individual too: it isn't really real. The self, the ego, the "I"—Hinduism's Atman—is but a wave on the ocean of Brahman; or rather, it's *a waving of* the ocean: not a thing discrete abiding on or beside the One, nor even really anything like a part of the Whole. Neither nominally nor mereologically substantial, the "I" is no thing but merely a word with which to designate an activity of the One, a mundane little verb existentially dependent on the Great Cosmic Noun. The apparent Many is really One, and the self drains away into the Universal Sea: Atman *is* Brahman.

Or call it energy, or force, or power. For we needn't divinize or anthropomorphize the One. It may be godlike, conscious and personal; but maybe not. We can only speculate as to its nature beyond the bare affirmations that *it is*; *it is one*; and *it generates plurality*. But who knows how it operates: Freely and deliberately? Or necessarily, by way of emission, emanation, or a ceaselessly spiraling fragmentation into fundamental elements? What can one say beyond the saying that the One does what It does?

Or does it? For maybe reality doesn't conform to the intellect's inclination to posit a unity as the source of multiplicity. Maybe the Many are fundamental and the One is a construct of consciousness. We are driven to seek simplicity behind complexity; and time and again we've succeeded in bringing diverse phenomena under the rule of strictly limited principles. But in no field have we ever reduced plurality to a single simple originary point. One wonders whether we could, in this case in particular: For a One all alone in its isolation would be barren, would it not? With what partner, by what means, from what motive would it spawn an other? Indeed, the thought sometimes intrudes: if ever there were only One, there never would be Many.

Must we insist on Many from the start, then? The imagined One is really Many? Maybe, but how many? And should we include in our reckoning the elements only, or forces too? And what about potentialities, dispositions, processes, and mechanisms? Oh, and selves—if there be Many, there must be a goodly many indeed of these:

an inexhaustible supply of "I"s. But, again, how many? I suppose we could say that the Many is precisely as many as required by theory to make sense of our experience, to "save the phenomena." This would appear the prudent attitude to adopt, the parsimonious approach. But to restrict our conclusions about the real to only what we can know of it, as if Being were subject to the propensities of the human intellect— well, this just seems exactly backward, or upside down.

Where then are we left? Staring at the blunt dead-end of a darkened alleyway. Or so it seems. For if we start with the One, it's a mystery how the Many has come to be. And if we start with the Many, we confront a series of equally vexing questions: How many? And why just *this* many, neither more nor less? And mustn't the Many comprise many things, which is to say many unities, many *ones*—but how is there any *one* at all if all there is is the Many?

Here we have the original version of the "Problem of the One and the Many." Which came first, unity or plurality? It's a particularly confounding conundrum because although there seem but two possible solutions, each one of them seems wrong.

So far I've put the problem in terms of Brahman, the One behind the apparent Many as formulated in Vedic Hinduism. But this text is a review primarily of selected scenes from the history of western philosophy. Let's turn then to those pondering men whose ruminations form the foundations of this tradition: let's attend to the Greeks.

2

Parmenides

Imagine there's only one thing. Not you, your imagination, and this thing. That's three things. I mean just a simple singularity, pure unity, and nothing else besides. Call it "the One."

Since the One is the only thing that *is*, the only thing to which the verb *to be* applies, we might also call it "That-Which-Is," or "Being"—as opposed to "That-Which-Is-Not," or "non-Being," or, well, "Nothing."

But now what about this Nothing that's opposed to Being? Is this some Second Thing in addition to the One? No, it's not; for since That-Which-Is-Not *is not*, since non-Being doesn't *be* and Nothing isn't anything at all, there's no other thing to be in addition to, or in opposition to, Being. Only That-Which-Is *is*. Only Being *be-s*. Nothing doesn't do anything; it doesn't even *noth*. It doesn't do—it *can't* do—because it doesn't *be*.

So there's Being and that's all there is. But is this "all there is" all that we can say about it: *that* it is? Can we say nothing about *what* it is? Actually, we *can* say something about this. We already have: we've said that Being is *one*. For imagine there being *two* instances of Being. What would there be between these two, separating them and rendering them distinct? It couldn't be some third thing, for that would only compound the problem: we'd wonder what separates the first from the second instances of Being, and then again what separates the second from the third. No, it makes no sense: Being cannot distinguish Being from Being. But what else could serve the purpose? Non-Being? Really? So non-Being is the thing between two instances of Being, distinguishing one from the other? But non-Being isn't a thing, so it's not there to be anywhere between any other things. No, none of this will do: neither Being nor non-Being will generate multiplicity from unity.

So if there's only Being and no Nothing, there must be only *one* Being, only one One, and this One must be all there is. And if we premise that all there is is this one thing, we can conclude that there isn't more than this, which is to say that there isn't a plurality of things. If there is only the One, then there is no Many.

But that's not all we can say. We can add that the One doesn't change: doesn't change place or properties or states. It doesn't enter into relations, with itself or anything else (there isn't anything else). Nor does it come to be or pass away.

If Being were to change, it would change into that which it previously was not, which is to say into non-Being. And if it were to move, it would move to a place where previously it was not, which is to say it would move into a void of non-Being. But since non-Being *is not*, there is no non-Being for Being to change, or to move, into. Similarly, if Being were to come to be or pass away, it would come to be from, or pass away into, non-Being. But, again, there isn't any non-Being for Being to come to be from or to pass away into.

In sum, That-Which-Is *is* and That-Which-Is-Not *is not*, and therefore Being is one, eternal, unchanging and unmoving, utterly unalterable and absolutely unique. Silent and still, pristinely serene, it is the All and Only. The solitary One.

This anyway seems to have been Parmenides' teaching, which with the aid of his disciple Zeno's paradoxes spread from his home in southern Italy throughout the Greek intellectual world like a steadily expanding glacier, freezing minds and tongues along its course. All is One: there's nothing more to say, and no one besides to say it.

You understand Parmenides' point, don't you? Of course you do: It's simple logic premised on the datum that there's no such thing as Nothing. It's indisputable. There exists one thing and one thing only: the One. But you worry that you don't *experience* this, that reality doesn't appear to you as one, as a simple singularity and nothing else besides. You see rather many complex things, coming and going, here and there, bursting into and blinking out of existence, objects expanding and contracting, containing and contained, filling up, flowing out, and rolling around at your feet. You see a frenzied multiplicity.

Or so you think. But maybe you're deluded, or dreaming, or under some kind of spell. In any case, argument and experience refuse to align in your mind. And this troubles you. Moreover, if there is only the One, there's no you independent of the One to try to understand it, nor any thoughts or words with which to articulate your understanding, or lack thereof. Every apparently distinct entity—things, minds, selves, ideas—is subsumed into the All. Coagulated. Congealed. And all this is a problem.

Or maybe *you*'re the problem. It's hard to say; impossible really to identify the precise source of confusion. After all, Parmenides was something of a mystagogue. He may well have been a healer-prophet (a *iatromantis*) who founded an incubation cult in which initiates lay alone in caves cloaked in mystic dark, silent and still, praying and awaiting divine visions.[1] He claims in the poem he wrote—that's right: he wrote a poem, not a treatise—he claims to have received his insights into Being from an unnamed goddess. So, yeah, it's likely we'll never know for sure what he was on about. But that's all right. That's just *aporia*, a paralyzing puzzlement generative of wonder. And that—well, that's philosophy.

---

[1] See Peter Kingsley's *In the Dark Places of Wisdom* (Golden Sufi, 1999).

3

Heraclitus

Can there be so many Many that there isn't any one? A multiplicity so extensive that it's not a collection of multiple units but a pure plurality? Imagine a field of flux in which the fluctuating subjects are themselves fluctuations, and every apparently finite simple dissolves upon inspection into an infinitude of infinities. Actions with no subjects, a whirl of noun-less verbs. The word for such a reality is Becoming, indicating interminable activity and change, aimless movement, in contrast to Parmenides' immobile Being. Here we have a reality devoid of unity, a world in which there is no One but only Many.

Only Many? Maybe we should change that to: *all-y* Many. Ha! Yes, maybe we should—but then again let's not. Probably there's no point. Heraclitus of Ephesus, like his opposite, Parmenides of Elea, is luring us beyond the limits of language; and it may well be that we can no more speak of pure Becoming than we can think of pure Being.

Nevertheless, being philosophers, we'll think as we please, and speak freely, today and evermore, if only to explore what becomes of our ideas.

Let's think then of strife and opposition, of conflagrations and cacophonies, violence and desire. Brightly unlike the equanimity of Parmenides' One, the Many of Heraclitus is (are) constantly in conflict with itself (themselves), extravagantly so, world without end. War is the father of all; discord is justice; and the thunderbolt steers all things.

From conflict comes creation. The brilliance of lightning flashes forth from contrary charges in a cloud; the purity of a single note sounds from a string stretched taut against the counter-force of a tuning peg; the stability of a chemical suspension—house paint, for example—derives from the disturbance of the compound's elements: to be still as one the many must be agitated.

Nor does all this happen randomly. For somewhere there is, behind or beneath or within the pandemonium—or at some time outside of time there comes to be, manifesting perhaps from the dynamism of the turmoil itself, by who knows what enchantment of generation—there is somehow a paradigm, a pattern, a rule. Heraclitus calls it the *logos*, and though academics toil in scholastic disputations over what exactly this might be, we may think of it as the configuring principle responsible for the order of the universe, a divine weaver (though not necessarily a divinity) eternally plaiting chaos into cosmos.

As pretty a pattern as may be, however, no configuration ever abides. All things are always changing in every way, and Being is but a mirage swaying in the vapors of Becoming. Plato presents this insight in his dialogue *Theaetetus*, in which he advances a reading of Heraclitus more radical by far than any other until Nietzsche's over two thousand years later.[1] As a young man Plato sat at the feet of Cratylus, a follower of Heraclitus so intense that at times he refused even to speak on the grounds that the very structure of language, with its stable subjects and objects, contradicts the nature of reality, which altogether lacks enduring substances. Heraclitus reportedly had remarked that a man can't step twice into the same river, because from one moment to the next the river changes; which insight Cratylus modified by insisting that a man can't step even once into the river, for in truth there is neither any man nor any river—for *there are no things*. In Plato's words, "nothing is one or something or any kind of thing . . . for nothing ever is but is always becoming" (*Theaetetus* 152d–e).

In sum, the Heraclitean ontology is altogether bereft of *onta* (beings). Strange to say, I know; but it's inescapable. And the consequences for language are equally startling: "The verb *to be* must be deleted altogether" (*Theaetetus* 157b). Crazy as this sounds, it's really only reasonable; for if nothing ever abides as any one thing, but "all things stream like waterways" (*Theaetetus* 160d), then there's nothing real about which we can say "*it is.*"

Note that this applies to *us*, too, every bit as much as to the objects supposedly surrounding us. We ourselves are caught up in the flow— more, we are dissolved and washed away. I am not I; you are not you; there is no he, she, or it. Socrates now and Socrates then, Socrates sitting and standing, healthy and ill, bearded and besheared—there is no enduring individual at the focus of these alterations, only a shifting multiplicity of momentary existents. Nor is there an enduring ego,

---

[1] An illuminating read is Nietzsche's lecture on Heraclitus in *The Pre-Platonic Philosophers* (University of Illinois, 2006), 53–74. It provides a glimpse of Nietzsche's early life as an academic philologist gifted with philosophical insight.

self, or psyche behind or within the flux to bind the multiplicity into unity. Genesis without terminus everlastingly, creation proceeds like a flame ignited and extinguished all but instantaneously, and repeatedly, enkindled then snuffed out again and again, and again, perpetually arising and passing away with such rapidity as to seem continuous—an apparent continuity which, as Nietzsche will later insist, is a *lie*.[2]

It probably goes without saying that it's hard to know what to make of Heraclitus. He certainly earned his ancient reputation as obscure. It doesn't help that we have only fragments of his book; but even the ancients who read the text entire were confounded by it. Given its oracular contents, it's fitting that after composing the work Heraclitus deposited the papyrus in the temple of Artemis. Let Apollo's shining sister make some sense of it.

As baffling as Heraclitus is all by himself, when we set Parmenides beside him we intensify our perplexity to the point of downright stupefaction. Can there really be only Being with no Becoming, or only Becoming without Being? Either option appears impotent to generate the world we see around us. Yet neither is it obvious how one might incorporate the two into a single worldview. Were the ontological flickerings of Heraclitean fire to liquify the frozen sphere of Parmenides' One, would the runoff douse the flame? Or can Becoming no more encounter Being than the riddling melancholiac stalking the grounds of the grand Ephesian temple could address the priestly poet communing with his goddess in distant Elea, the broad Mediterranean swelling between them?

I don't know. Who can say for sure? And with that we're back to *aporia*, and further entangled in philosophy.

---

[2] *Twilight of the Idols*, "Reason in Philosophy" 2.

4

Gorgias

Gorgias the sophist composed a treatise on non-Being. Of course he did. No one knows exactly why: some say to parody Parmenides; others say as a refutation. Maybe he was moved by a burst of rhetorical exuberance. In any case, Gorgias hailed from Leontini in Sicily, not far from Parmenides' home in southern Italy; so it's plausible to suggest that he had the Eleatics in mind. His thesis seems to be that non-Being *be-s*—That-Which-Is-Not *is*—but then again no it isn't; also that Being, That-Which-Is, is neither generated nor ungenerated, neither one nor many, neither—well, all that's the least of it: That-Which-Is *is not*, he says. Being *does not be*; it doesn't exist. And even if it does exist, no one can comprehend it. And even if we could comprehend it, we couldn't communicate it.

Some say this is nihilism, or skepticism at best. It's impossible now to say. We don't have the original work, so who really knows what Gorgias was up to? The sophists were a slippery lot; they came in every variety, from reactionary relativists to objectivist antinomians, from atheists to mystics. So let's keep to what we know, or sort of know, namely, Plato's view of Gorgias and his acolytes. In the dialogue Plato named after him, Gorgias is pictured as lodging with friends in Athens, offering his services for hire as a teacher, when Socrates pays a visit with a friend who hopes to study with him. Many young men are present too, ambitious sons of aristocrats, no doubt. More potential disciples. The dialogue enacts something like a battle for the souls of these youth—will they recognize in Socrates the merits of the philosophical life, or will they fall for Gorgias' suite of meretricious seductions?

To Socrates' request that he explain what it is he does, and what he'll teach to those who enroll with him, Gorgias, in a long, florid discourse, promises his students power, the power to acquire whatever they want and to act however they please, without shying away from vice or crime, and with no fear of punishment. In short, with no respect for justice. This last revelation, though, Gorgias doesn't exactly volunteer; he rather lets it slip. And when Socrates calls attention to it, Gorgias recoils: he's ashamed and, trying to walk it back, he contradicts a remark he'd made in the course of his speech. A contradiction? This is extraordinary: Gorgias had earlier boasted that he could reply skillfully to any question put to him; but Socrates has exposed him as unjust and dialectically inferior (*Gorgias* 455a–461b). What will the young men watching think?

We needn't review the dialogue in detail. Suffice it to say that Gorgias yields his place in the debate to one and then another of his students, Polus and Callicles. These men—Polus more than Gorgias, and Callicles more than Polus—exhibit a shockingly candid boldness: they're explicitly disdainful of shame, and frank in their esteem for injustice. They admire power; they desire pleasure; and that's pretty much the extent of their life's aspirations. Socrates for his part insists that by living thus they'll suffer, if not from the reproach of their fellows or punishment by the authorities, then from the penalty of living a bad life or, worse still, dying into a tortured afterlife.

Polus and Callicles are unmoved. Gorgias too, one assumes. The teaching of oratory is how he earns his living, after all; and he's old and accustomed to fine things. He craves the wealth and recognition. But what about the noble young men in attendance? The eager audience, what's their assessment? They've just witnessed Socrates' intellectual acuity and verbal dexterity firsthand; he's unquestionably superior to his opponents, even when engaging on their own field of battle. And the field of Socrates' activity is more expansive and handsomer than theirs, nobler even than all the plains of regal or martial glory, beautiful though these are. Socrates understands: in his life he's experienced power, pleasure, violence, and glory, and still he's sure that the goodness of virtue surpasses them all.[1] Goodness, of which men like Callicles know little and care less.

Callicles is beyond the traditions of good and evil. He conducts himself "naturally" (according to *physis*, the way things are in the wild, as it were), contrary to convention (*nomos*, the adventitious manners of cities and men). In this he's unusual among his peers, and a prefiguring of Nietzsche. It's not that he's a nihilist, strictly speaking, nor even a relativist; he's the type I named earlier an "objectivist antinomian," which is not unlike the man (himself, in particular) that Nietzsche will call an "immoralist." In *On the Genealogy of Morals*,

---

[1] Socrates fought as a hoplite solider, on more than one occasion. He even saved the fallen Alcibiades on the front lines at Potidaea, for the bravery of which the younger man nominated him to be officially honored. (For more on Socrates' military career and its implications for his ethical views, see my "Socrates as Hoplite," *Ancient Philosophy* 25 (2005): 273–89.)

Nietzsche wrote that when he titled his previous book *Beyond Good and Evil*, he didn't mean "Beyond Good and Bad" ("First Essay" 17). Callicles would approve this quip. Like Nietzsche, he lives by exacting principles and something like a code of honor; he holds to values he'll neither relativize nor abandon. But, also like Nietzsche, he'll not stoop to trying to "ground" his values in tales about the metaphysical truth of Being. This is the element of the outlook of (some of) the sophists that Nietzsche had in mind when he praised them as "realists."

But the sophists weren't all realists or eccentric objectivists. The paradigmatic sophist, Protagoras, is the paradigmatic relativist. "Man is the measure of all things," he said. Which is to say that reality has no nature in and of itself, independent of our perceptions of it; it bends with our beliefs.

Whether objectivist or relativist, in one way or another, the typical sophist denied the great pyramidal hierarchy of Being that for Platonists grounds reality, truth, and value. Regardless of their personal beliefs, the sophists' influence on the public was to undermine the citizens' confidence in the rightness of a city's laws, whether natural or divine. Plato's own cousin, Critias, made the case that the gods are fictions concocted by the founders of cities to add gravitas to their dicta and their laws. And Plato himself, in his *Republic*, to prove that the just is superior to the unjust life must argue not only that the gods exist but that they judge us by the merits of our actions. All of which is to say, to resist the sophistic spirit of the late fifth century was to argue for objective standards as measures of man's activity.

Any such argument, to succeed, must build on the ground of Being. Being is truth; Being is the real; Being is *that which is*. Mere opinions won't do, subjectivity, points of view, perspectives: these things bow and blow with the breeze. From Asia to Europe, Athens to Sparta, from Socrates to Democritus and Plato to Nietzsche, the winds of opinion shake the leaves of place and time, sweeping ever on, changing minds. That'll get you somewhere, but nowhere for long; it'll whirl you around among the ephemera of Becoming, but it won't settle you down on the permanent truths of Being.

5

One and Many

Stop reading, look around, and ask yourself: with what types of things is reality populated? Very generally, I mean. So don't answer, "with *people* and *trees* and *stars* and *clouds* . . ." Rather, expand your conceptual categories and reply with something more abstract like, "with spatio-temporal objects." Such a formulation encompasses people and trees and stars and clouds—and, well, everything else you observe around you now. At first glance, anyway.

So, yes, whichever way you direct your gaze you encounter individual three-dimensional objects, discrete and self-contained. Material bodies; physical substances. Now consider the following fundamental property of such things: they occupy space and time in such a way that each one can be in only a single place at any specific moment of time. No material body can be both here and there simultaneously. The book or tablet you're presently reading, for example, can *only* be *here* in your hands or *there* on the desk (or wherever it happens to be) *right now*; it can't *also* be in another room *at the same time*—not anyway unless you cut or break it in two, and then only half of it will be in each location.

This just is what it is to be a material object, this thing here or that thing there: each thing is identical to itself, independent of every other thing, localized in space and time, and particularized in being. Ok, good; but now ask yourself: Does any other kind of thing exist? A kind perhaps that isn't so strictly bounded and isolated from every other thing? A kind that *can* be in many places at one time? If so, it would have to be something other than a material individual.

Forget for now the spatio-temporal dimensionality that's so basic as to be common to all material objects. There are other properties—many other properties—that material objects don't all share. Specific shapes, for example. Of course, every material object has a shape; but their shapes differ. In some cases, anyway; in some cases they're identical. Your book or tablet is probably a rectangle, and so most likely are the door to your room, your bed, and your driver's license. Most of the other objects in your immediate environment aren't rectangular; but these are, and some others are too. But now consider this shape, this rectangularity: it's odd, isn't it? It exists in many places at one time, but it's not divided into separate parts. All of rectangularity—the whole of it, one hundred percent—is in your book. If it weren't, your book wouldn't be fully a rectangle. But all of rectangularity is also in your door, your bed, and your ID card. It's not just here, it's also there, and there, and there, and all at the same time. And since rectangularity obviously isn't nothing, it's something; but it's something of a kind other than a spatio-temporal material object.

What is it, then, this rectangularity? What kind of thing? And of what kind are all the other properties that manifest in many places at one time—the yellow that's common to the sun and the daisy; the human nature you share with all people everywhere; the beauty of a landscape, a melody, and your beloved's face? Traditionally, these kinds have been designated "universals."

In contrast to the "individuals" or "particulars" that are material objects, "universals" are neither composed of matter nor subject to spatio-temporal restrictions. They are real features of the world—for surely we aren't just imagining rectangularity and human nature—but they aren't quite "things" either, anyway they're not material things. So, if we were to draw up an inventory of the furniture of the universe, we'd have to include at least two types of things or realities: material particulars and immaterial universals.

Here we approach a variation on the problem of the One and the Many. Of any one kind of thing—human, for example—there are many individual instances. There's only one nature or paradigm of human, but there are very many human beings. The one—the very same and self-identical one, *human nature*—manifests in each of the many, and by doing so configures them all as humans. So—and to change examples—the one nature of sphericity manifests in the sun, as does the nature of heat and the nature of yellow, and thereby is the sun configured as a spherical, hot, yellow object. Yet each one of these natures manifests simultaneously in many other things besides the sun: sphericity in basketballs, marbles, and the earth; heat on and around a lighted match or a running engine; yellow in a traffic light or a baby chicken.

The problem is what to make of the "ontological status" of these different types of reality. Which is to say: in what exactly does their reality consist? Regarding material things the question is easy to answer: they exist as particular spatio-temporal objects subject to the laws of physics and accessible to us by our senses. Universals aren't like this at all. We don't experience them directly in and of themselves, but only as they're embodied in material individuals. Yet neither do they resemble fictional entities like unicorns or Sherlock Holmes. No one has ever seen rectangularity with his eyes, but we've all experienced it as manifest in rectangular objects; and it certainly doesn't seem that we have "made it up." What are these universals, then? We've agreed that they're real, but of what sort is their reality? And how exactly do they relate to, manifest in, and configure the individuals that embody them? This is the problem of the ontological status of universals, a problem for which Plato provides an infamous solution.

6

Plato

Ontology

Recall Parmenides' Being, the All and Only, the ungenerated, incorruptible, motionless, and unalterable One. No one really understands what Parmenides had in mind with the name he gave to this . . . this . . . whatever it is. Anyway, the expression he employed in Greek is *to eon*. Plato later adopted the term (in its linguistically mature form, *to on*) for his own speculations about the One and the Many and the ontological status of universals. The intellectual world would never be the same: these two little words, this slight and unassuming "*to on*," would come to be quite possibly the most consequential subject in the history of western philosophy, perhaps of philosophy globally. Considering the stakes, we should at least try to make some sense of it.

It's not particularly difficult to translate the expression. The *to* is the definite article, "the"; the *on* is the present participle of the verb *einai*, which means "to be"; the case is nominative and the gender is neuter. So the unadorned literal translation is, "the is-ing thing," or "the being thing," hence the standard rendering of "Being." With the capital letter—you were wondering why the capital "B," weren't you?—with this we try to capture the oddity implied by the use of the definite article. Employed as a participle in a standard sentence, the word "being" isn't in the least problematic: "I, John Smith, being of sound mind and body, do hereby declare etc." But removed from this context and outfitted with a definite article, the word no longer functions adjectivally to introduce a participial clause; rather, it's transformed into a substantive, as we might extract the verb "to run" from the sentence, "John, running home after work, feared he would arrive too late," and by affixing to it a definite article, make of it a substantive, thus: "the running man." Such expressions as "the running man" or "the flying nun" present no difficulties of comprehension—but "the is-ing thing"?, "the being thing"? These formulations are inescapably strange. What should one denominate a thing principally characterized by the fact that it *is* or that it *be-s*? "That-Which-Is" comes close, though it doesn't express the participial sense. "The Is-ing Thing" comes closer, but it's too peculiar. And to go with "Is-ing" all by itself really is to go too far. Hence, for good or ill: Being.

But still there's the question of how to understand the "is" at issue here. The verb "to be" may be used in a number of different ways: there's the veridical use according to which "it is" signifies "it is true" or "it is the case"; there's the locative use for "it is here"; there's the copulative for assigning a predicate to a subject, as in "Plato is Athenian"; and there's the existential use by which we posit something in reality in contrast to non-being: "Plato is" = "Plato exists." There are others, but these will do for our purposes. Now, as I've said, we don't know exactly what Parmenides had in mind: all that we have from him are fragments of a single short and mystifying poem. Fortunately, from Plato we have more, much more. But I'll spare you a rehearsal of the evidence and argumentation and state in brief that Plato's conceptualization of *einai* in his use of *to on* seems to be primarily copulative, employed to predicate specific characteristics of a given subject: "x is just" or "x is beautiful."

Do you follow? Does all that make sense? If not, don't worry. Just forget all those words and know that when Plato writes of Being—or when I write of Plato writing of Being—you should take the word as a synonym for "essence"—essence being that collection of properties that makes a thing to be the kind of thing it is; or, to put it the other way around, those properties without which a thing must cease to be the kind of thing it is. The essence of a triangle, for example, is a shape with three sides, three angles, and three vertices; the essence of a bachelor is a man who's never been married; and the essence of water is an inorganic compound having one oxygen and two hydrogen atoms.

Essential properties are necessary properties; any particular thing will have any number of other properties that aren't essential, and therefore not necessary: color the triangle red or blue, make it large or small, place it here or there: it's still a triangle; whatever age or height or ethnicity of the unmarried man, he's still a bachelor; and whether the H_2O is in your refrigerator, falling from the sky, or frozen on the surface of a lake, it's still water. But add an angle to the triangle, marry off the bachelor, remove one of the hydrogen atoms from the H_2O—and you no longer have a triangle, a bachelor, or water.

It's important to go through all this because essence plays a crucial role in Plato's philosophy. It's the One in his account of the One and the Many, and it's the universal responsible for many individuals being one kind of thing. The nature of human or of rectangularity, as discussed in the previous chapter as that which by manifesting in a thing configures it as a human or a rectangle—this "nature" is just another way of saying "essence."

And there's another way of saying both, Plato's way: Form. You've no doubt heard of "Plato's theory of Forms." Plato's Forms are essences—or call them natures, kinds, divine blueprints, or perfect exemplars: we could argue about the subtle distinctions suggested by these different terms, but we won't. I employ them indiscriminately to give you a rough idea of what Plato has in mind.[1]

So Plato is an essentialist, which is to say that he contends that individuals are enformed by natures (essences) that render them abidingly the kinds of things they are. And, as I've said, these natures infuse the things they enform with a note of necessity: change a thing's nature, alter any one of its essential properties, and it will no longer be the same kind of thing.

So this is what we mean by essences. But what to make of their ontological status? Are essences real beings of some unusual variety—immaterial entities that manifest in many different things at the same time and somehow cause them to express this or that set of necessary properties; or are they nothing in themselves but rather only concepts, mental constructs that we project onto things in our classificatory schemes; or maybe they aren't even that, for maybe

---

[1] Similarly, we may say of the material particulars that they "participate in" the Forms (this is the usual technical term), or that they "partake of," "exemplify," "imitate," or "are imperfect copies of" the Forms. Each expression implies a specific understanding of the relationship between particulars and Forms, but we need not go into such detail. In this text I employ words ("embody," for instance) that I hope will be easy enough to understand in a general sense.

our minds don't actually contrive such general concepts—maybe all we do when we speak of essences is to deploy "kind-words" for ease of communication. These three rival interpretations are known as realism, conceptualism, and nominalism.

Plato is most emphatically a realist about essences. The Platonic Forms are objectively real beings. They cannot be reduced to mere concepts or vocabulary items concocted for convenience. They are in fact the *most* real beings of all, more real even than the things—the many material objects—they enform. Collectively Plato refers to the Forms as *ta onta*, the plural of *to on*. Thus they are *the is-ing things*, the ultimate beings, the things that most actually and truly *are*. The Forms, in short, are the *really real*.

When I say that the Forms most really and truly *are*, you must not take this existentially to indicate that they really exist—though of course they do exist—but take it rather predicatively to emphasize that *they truly are what they are without deviation*. The Form of x is not simultaneously, or later, or in other circumstances or from another perspective also something else; it's not not-x, say, or y. Each Form is always only absolutely itself.

But wait . . . Earlier I noted that essence or Form functions as the One in Plato's account of the One and the Many; but just now I've written of "Forms," in the plural. What gives? Well, Plato is no Parmenides, believing only in the one and only One. He accepts the reality of the Many; in fact, he insists upon an abundant multitude of material objects. But he's no Heraclitus either: there's a place in his system—a preeminent place—for more than just the Many, specifically for the idea of pure unity, for the One. In this way Plato reconciles Parmenides with Heraclitus. Sort of.

So, yes, there are many Forms, as there are many material objects; but each Form is a One in relation to the Many of its instantiations. There is only one Form of *human*, for example, but many instantiations of it in the billions of past, present, and future human beings. There is one Form of *beauty*, one Form of *justice*, and one Form of (mathematical) *equality*, and so on, while there are many beautiful sights and sounds, many just deeds, and many equal quantities. For each of the many natural kinds of thing there is one, and only one, corresponding Form whose presence to or in the things renders them members of their specific kind.

There may well be for Plato also another, a higher, indeed a supreme One, referred to in *Republic* Book 6 as "the unhypothetical first principle of all" (511b) and associated with "the Idea of the Good" (508e). But as he never writes of this principle explicitly and at length, perhaps reserving its explication for his "unwritten doctrines," there isn't much more we can say about it here.[2] Therefore we'll stay focused on the Forms.

---

[2] See the footnote on p. 56.

7

Plato

Epistemology

If it's true, as Plato tells it in the *Phaedrus*, that the Forms are "beyond the heavens" and "colorless, shapeless, and intangible" (247c), how could we ever know them? If they really are so thoroughly incorporeal, they must also be inaccessible to the senses. And that's right; the senses know nothing of the Forms. But Plato doesn't regard the senses as sources of knowledge to begin with. The senses admit sights and sounds generative of opinion only. Knowledge comes from the intellect alone.

Every schoolboy knows the "Allegory of the Cave" from Book 7 of Plato's *Republic*. Here the philosopher likens Forms to real things in the world beyond the cave, but material objects he compares to shadows cast on an interior wall by a fire ablaze near the cave's entrance. The image conveys the idea that whereas the Forms are truly and abidingly themselves, being real and enduring substances, physical objects are constantly changing like insubstantial phantasms. Recall the second and third chapters of this book, and take note: each Form possesses the characteristics of Parmenides' One (each is a perfect eternal and unchanging unity); and all material objects are always changing in every way, just like Heraclitus' swirling sea of Becoming.

Much less familiar than Plato's Cave is the image of the so-called "Divided Line" in *Republic* Book 6. By way of the Line Plato draws ontological distinctions between material things and immaterial Forms, as he does in the Cave; but he also stresses corresponding epistemological points. Take a line and divide it in half, he says; then divide each of the halves in half again. This procedure generates four sections, within each of which Plato sets a cognitive state, ranking the four from lowest to highest according to their degree of clarity or certainty, which is, in turn, derived from the ontological status of their objects. At the bottom of the scale is "imaging" (*eikasia*), by which we're acquainted with images like shadows and reflections in water. Above this is "opinion" or "belief" (*pistis*), which is the cognitive state produced by the senses whose objects are physical things. In the upper two sections of the Line are ratiocination (*dianoia*), by which we reason our way to knowledge of mathematical truths, and, highest and purest of all, understanding (*noêsis*), which is the crystalline apprehension of Form.

Today we're inclined to say that material things are the only proper objects of knowledge (studied by science), whereas any ostensibly immaterial reality can only be a matter of belief (the fancy of philosophical or theological speculation). From Plato's perspective this is precisely upside down—and he'd insist that we're the ones standing on our heads, not him.

I've written that material objects are constantly changing, but their ontological instability is even more radical than this implies. Unlike Forms, which are perfect, eternal, unchanging, and always and only exactly what they are, material objects are imperfect reflections of the Forms that enform them, they come to be and pass away, they change (of course), and—perhaps most strikingly of all—they possess contrary properties at one and the same time. A thing like an oak tree, for example, is large compared to a rooster, but small beside a mountain; a hummingbird is fast compared to a snail, but slow in relation to the speed of light; the number four is a double of the number two, but only half of eight. Thus entangled in intricate networks of associations and relationships, material objects never stay put as this or that in and of themselves; they can only be characterized and classified in contrast with or comparison to other things. From surface to core every material individual is shot through with branching fissures of relativity.

It's all these features of physical things—from temporal impermanence to property-relativity—that prevent them from being proper objects of knowledge. There's nothing stable about them for the intellect to grasp and know. This is their flux, and it goes all the way down, and that which fluctuates with such perpetual and varied motion can never be caught, much less held. So although we can state that this material thing, from this particular perspective, in relation to these other material things, at this moment, in this context, as considered by this person in this condition, appears to be x—although we can characterize a material thing with the addition of such qualifications, we cannot state simply and finally what it is in and of itself. Because *it isn't anything in and of itself*. Only a Form is stable in this way: *auto kath' auto*, as Plato regularly expresses the matter: itself according to itself.

So the world of material objects that's accessible to our senses is the realm of opinion or belief. We perceive these things, and we formulate beliefs about them; but these perceptions and beliefs no more get at Truth than do the countless other actual and possible perceptions and beliefs of the countless other subjects who confront the world from their own points of view. And please do keep in mind: the problem isn't with us. We can't get at the truth of material things because *there is no truth in them.*

Forms alone are knowable because only in them is there truth, non-relative, abiding, certain, and perspicuous truth. But there's still the question of *how* we know them. And although it pains me to say this, I admit that Plato's reply may not be entirely satisfactory to everyone presently reading this book. It will be especially objectionable to the typical modern materialist. But it must be said, so let's just say it without evasion or circumlocution, then afterward I'll essay a brief *apologia* for Plato's approach to the matter.

Ok, so here it goes: We come to know the Forms when we dwell among them after death during the interval before our next incarnation. Yes, according to Plato, the soul is immortal, and death is the separation of the soul from the mortal body until such time as it is born again into another body as another person. And since soul is the seat of the intellect and body the housing of the senses, in death the intellect has access to the Forms unimpeded by the confused and confusing input of the bodily organs. The *pure subject of knowledge*—the intellect, which Plato calls "the pilot of the soul"—in the unmediated presence of the *pure objects of knowledge*—the Forms, which he labels "the paradigm[s] of true knowledge" (*Phaedrus* 247c)—utterly liberated from any admixture of the fluctuating material realm, contemplates the Forms directly and thereby comes to know their truth.

Strange, I know; and we're not done yet. When the soul is reborn it's stocked with knowledge acquired as I have just described. But being born into a new body, it is from the very moment of birth overwhelmed with the incessant influx of sensory information about the material world, and, thus swamped by the waters of Becoming, the soul forgets its pure knowledge of Being. Yet with the proper nurturing and education a soul may recover some, or even all, of its pre-natal knowledge, and this is what we call "learning"; really, though, what's actually happening is "remembering," or "recollection."[1]

Don't say I didn't warn you. But in Plato's defense, consider that he's dealing with a vexing problem that worries us to this day. He wants to explain so-called "innate knowledge." At issue is whether—and, if so, to what extent—we are born pre-programmed and equipped, as it were, with knowledge or organizing cognitive structures. Some parties to this debate insist that we're born as "blank slates" and that, therefore, all knowledge comes only from experience. We'll explore this idea in greater detail later; for now, suffice it to say that if we start with the assumption of an utterly empty, purely receptive mind, it's impossible that we should ever acquire indubitable knowledge. Plato was sure that we do have knowledge, even if it's inaccessible until a master educator coaxes it into consciousness—mathematics is perhaps the most persuasive example of this. And, he thought, if we do in fact have knowledge of necessary truths, since this can't come from experience, we must have acquired it prior to experience. And since we begin to experience at birth, we must have acquired it prior

---

[1] For a concise account of the doctrine that learning is recollection, see *Phaedo* 72e–77a.

to birth. Hence his doctrines of pre-natal knowledge and "learning as recollection."

I could fill out the picture of the life of the soul during the interval of death, describing its nature and its mode of associating with the Forms; but Plato tends to alter the details from dialogue to dialogue. This is all for the best, I say. For I take his variations on this theme to imply that he isn't actually committed to the specifics, and that he includes them only as provocative suggestions designed to enhance the artistry of his work and to stimulate his readers' thoughts. He's committed to there being Forms, the immaterial essences of material things; and he's sure that they're intelligible and that, given the appropriate conditions, guidance, and training, we humans can come to know them; and he's confident that we apprehend them through the pure contemplative activity of intellect, not through sensory experience. It's likely that he also believes that the soul is immortal and, further, that it acquires knowledge of truth when separated from the body in the state we call death. A belief in the transmigration of the soul was common to the esoteric intellectual and spiritual traditions of Plato's day, Pythagoreanism in particular, which seems to have had some influence on Plato's thinking. So perhaps it's to be expected that he would draw on the idea to explain the mysterious fact that we humans seem to possess knowledge prior to, and independent of, sensory experience. But, as I say, I doubt he thought he understood the matter in any more detail than this. In any case, I certainly don't.

8

Plato

Objectivism and Relativism

In his *Theaetetus* Plato associates the Heraclitean doctrine of total flux—there are no islands of Being in the universal sea of Becoming—with Protagoras' radical relativism (truth is whatever one believes it to be). An influential intellectual and the original sophist, an older contemporary of Socrates, Protagoras of Abdera taught that "man is the measure of all things," by which he meant, as we have seen, that opinion is the sole standard of truth. If nothing abides as a fact common to all; if reality itself varies according to each individual's experience; then every man's perception of the world must be accurate for him. There being no data independent of his experience against which to measure his perceptions, there's no other way it could be (151e–160e).

Every man's perception is accurate *for him*. Or: for her, for me, for them. Like today's ubiquitous expressions, "my truth," "your truth," "their reality," and so on, all such formulations are fundamentally relativistic, for they imply that truth or reality is what it is *only in relation to*—or *relative to*—what someone takes it to be. Likewise, the popular rhetorical question: "Who's to say?" If there's a locution more overworked in discussions of ethics today than this, I don't know what it is. And it's meant to imply that no one *can* affirm definitively what's right or wrong, good or bad, just or unjust, etc., because there's no definitive fact of the matter about such things. It's all subjective.

Plato had no use for this way of thinking. He was, and he remains, the western world's premiere objectivist. Truth *is*, and *it is what it is*, independently of anyone's thoughts about it or experience of it. Truth is absolute because reality itself is determinate and fixed—some features of the real, anyway; namely, the Forms. And since Forms enform many aspects of our world, not just metaphysical and mathematical reality but also, for example, the nature of man and of human virtue (wisdom, justice, temperance, courage, piety, etc.)—since this is so, ethical matters are objective too. More, since, given the facts of human nature, we can say that the good life is the virtuous life, we can conclude that the good life for a human isn't a matter of personal opinion, relative and mutable; it's objective, stable, and knowable. Who's to say what's a good human life? The person who knows what it is to be a human, that's who; which is to say, the person who understands the invariable facts of human nature.

So Platonism is a thoroughly objectivist philosophy—there are real, mind-independent, certain, and invariant truths to be discovered in the fields of ontology, epistemology, politics, ethics, and aesthetics—because the reality investigated by these disciplines just is what it is, and what it is doesn't depend on us. Man is not the measure of all things. He may at times be one who measures, a judge of his or others' opinions; but the criterion of the accuracy of his measurement is, and always will be, the world as it is independent of his judgment.

It's true there are serious questions about whether, and how, we can ever come to know the world as it is in itself, independent of our experience. But, despite the timeless undergraduate refrain that people, cultures, and, yes, even entire civilizations organize their lives around irreconcilably divergent opinions about reality, religion, and how to live—their "measurements" differ, so who's to say who's right?—despite the popularity of the observation, it has no bearing whatever on whether there's objective truth. It's simple logic, actually: the phenomenon of disagreement, even passionate, unresolvable disagreement, implies precisely nothing about the objective reality of the matter in dispute; and it most definitely doesn't suggest that there isn't any such reality.

Consider this: In the ancient world, when some people believed the earth to be a sphere while others thought it barrel-shaped or flat like a disc, was the earth no shape at all? Or was it simultaneously several different shapes, as many as there were opinions about it? The question is ridiculous, and this is so because disagreement (or agreement, for that matter) has no bearing on truth.

"But there's a difference," you reply, "between the shape of the earth and this business about virtue and the good life. We can verify the shape of the earth—we've circumnavigated the seas and orbited the globe. There's GPS and satellites! There's video! We can see with our own eyes that the earth's a sphere!"

So the earth had no shape, or it had multiple shapes simultaneously, in the past, but now it's a sphere because we can verify it empirically?

"No, that's not what I mean at all. In the past we didn't have the resources to verify it; but it was verifiable in principle. Even two thousand years ago the earth was the sort of thing that *could* be orbited; we just lacked the technology to do it."

Now we're entering perilous territory. Fortunately for us, these wastelands were explored and mapped long ago. I won't bother with a detailed history; you can study for yourself the controversies regarding "the principle of verification." For now, I'll just remark that if you mean to assert that only that which can be verified empirically counts as real or true, then you'll have to ask yourself what's implied by the fact that that very proposition can't be empirically verified. You see? The principle fails to satisfy its own criterion of truth; so it's self-defeating. Therefore, it can't do the rational work you'd like it to do.

But you persist: "Okay, I see your point. But even if verifiability won't do as a general criterion of truth, it's not nothing. It still seems significant that since everyone can see the shape of the earth, we can all agree about it—whoever dissents is just a willfully ignorant crank. But even normal rational people can't agree about virtue and the good life because no one can prove their assertions about these things. There's no evidence. So it all just seems subjective."

But when you say that we can't "prove" these things, you assume that empirical verification is the sole proper mode of proof. Why should we believe that? Besides, you're now just restating your previous claim that if we can't agree about something, it's subjective. But that still doesn't follow. And this is so whether we're reasoning about the shape of the earth or the nature of virtue or beauty—the fact that we can't set a yardstick against the object of interest changes nothing.

Finally, think about it this way: our *beliefs about* morality are relative to our experience, education, and cultural norms; they're subjective. But that's true too of our beliefs about mathematics and physics—it's true of *all* beliefs, because beliefs just are subjective states of mind. The question of relativism isn't the question whether our *beliefs about* x are subjective—of course they are; that's just the nature of a belief—the question is whether the *objects of our beliefs*—x itself and its nature—are subjective or objective. We're particularly prone to confuse these questions when thinking about morality because the term can be understood in two different senses: it can refer to either our *beliefs about* what's right and wrong (which are indeed subjective) or to the *facts* about what *really is* right and wrong (which, if there are such facts, are objective). So, yes, different cultures have different moralities—using "morality" in the first sense, as a codified collection of *beliefs about* right and wrong—and that's unlikely to change. But we want to know whether, apart from these diverse moral codes, there's "morality" in the second sense, namely, a *moral truth* about which one or some of these codes are correct and the others mistaken.

Does that make sense? I imagine it does, right now, just after I've explained it; but don't be surprised if you find yourself reverting to your old, sloppy way of thinking very soon—it happens with my students all the time. I point out that disagreement doesn't prove absence of truth; they understand—because, frankly, it's elementary—yet come the next day they insist on moral relativism because, well, different cultures think differently about these things, so who's to say who's right!

Sad to say, but this sort of slipshod thinking is widespread and habitual. Still, give the following a try: whatever your opinion about truth and objectivity, please at least make an effort to put out of your mind the fallacious but pervasive pseudo-argument that since people disagree about x, there's no fact of the matter about it.

But to conclude by restating the central theme of the present chapter: Platonism is strictly objectivist, and this is so because it affirms the reality of Being, specifically as essences, natures, or—in Platonist jargon—Forms. Some stable ground of Being is required if we're to anchor truth against the rushing currents of Becoming. Hence, Forms. And to look ahead: it's the gradual erosion and deterioration of Being, the forgetting and finally the emphatic rejection of even the very idea of Being—culminating in Nietzsche's Heraclitean celebration of "the innocence of Becoming"—that shepherded the West from Platonism to nihilism.

9

One and Many

How is it that many things can be one thing? And why is it that, although in many cases many things are one thing, in other cases many things are nothing more, or less, than many things? How can one of the many things that while many are also one change with respect to many of its properties while yet remaining one? For doesn't it sometimes also happen that so many properties of some one thing change that it becomes many from having been one? And in such cases, are each of these new many things now one, and, if so, can each one of these many new things change again in many ways while yet remaining one, and can they also change in so many ways that they become many new ones in their turn?

Let's think about unity—not in the abstract, but as we encounter it in the physical world. Organisms, objects, things. A human, for instance. Each of us as an individual is a complex collection of parts—limbs, tissues, organs, cells, molecules, atoms. These parts aren't particularly stable either: we're forever shedding and regrowing skin cells; the cells of the tissues that compose our organs regularly degenerate and die, are repaired or replaced; the molecules of our cells are composed of atoms that, really, we probably shouldn't even regard as unified "things." At every level this assemblage of parts intermingles with the surrounding environment—we inhale oxygen and other chemicals and incorporate them into our bodies; photons entering our eyes are absorbed as energy; the atoms on the surface of our skin interact with the atoms of the air around us, the clothes we wear, the furniture on which we sit. If we could observe the world at the subatomic level, would it even be apparent where our organism ends and our surroundings begin—the boundary, say, between the surface of our skin and the ambient air, or another person whose skin is pressed against our own? It's not obvious that the line between us would be so well-defined.

Yet we *are* distinct from our surroundings. I, as a thing, as a unified entity, do not include the air around me or the chair on which I sit. You too, of course. You're most likely holding a book or a tablet, your hands gripping it firmly; yet the book is not a part of you: you're an independent entity. But consider a sculpture of someone holding a book—in this case the person and the book constitute a single continuous thing. Why is our case different? In a world that at the micro-level seems a buzzing confusion of intersecting waves, how exactly are there any stark lines and demarcations?

I assume you take yourself to be the same you who was born however many years ago you were born, also that you expect it to be the same you who will pass away so very, very many (let us hope!) years from now. But how can this be? Think how much you've changed since you were born. Everything about your physical constitution is different—your height, weight, skin tone, hair color, the very shape of your limbs. And your mind: you have different sentiments now, different sensations, other thoughts and beliefs, emotions, desires, and fears; you have altogether different memories, dreams, and reflections. Moreover, most of the matter that constitutes you as an organism has been replaced more than once since you were born—and as for those cells or groups of cells that remain the same: I doubt you locate your personal identity there, in some persistent membrane-bound molecules. What is it, then, that makes you you, one and the same you despite so many changes?

And please don't say it's your DNA. DNA is another complex structure, subject to the very questions we've been asking. What is it that makes these many molecules one organic chemical? Yes, they're joined by bonds of shared electrons of the atoms that compose them; but, again, this only replicates the problem—what constitutes the atoms as a molecule; the protons, neutrons, and electrons as an atom; the quarks as protons and neutrons? The bonds and forces involved—apart from the possibility that they're only placeholders for explanations we don't have—are the means by which the individual is held together; but they don't account for the phenomenon of individuality itself.

The Buddhists teach a doctrine of "co-dependent origination," according to which all things are so intertwined as to not be independent things at all. Any "one" thing is causally dependent on many others for its very existence; it's mereologically dependent because it is what it is as a whole in relation to some other things regarded as its parts, while it also functions as a part of some larger system or process; and, finally, it's conceptually dependent to the extent that its very identity hangs on our conceptualizing it as such—we carve it out from its surroundings, as it were, by the modes of operation of our perceptual and cognitive systems. The apparent unity of the individual, then, is in reality a multiplicity; and we mistake for independent entities what are in fact but nodes of an infinitely interwoven net.

Nietzsche will later develop similar ideas, insisting for example that the very concept "thing" is a construct of reason reinforced by the "metaphysics of language" (TI "Reason" 5). When the Buddhists insist that all "things" are characterized by an emptiness (*shunyatâ*) of intrinsic nature or self-nature (*svabhâva*), they are in effect anticipating Nietzsche's denial of "thinghood" or "substance," a denial that strikes at the very heart of classical western philosophy, particularly the ontology most thoroughly articulated by Aristotle.

10

Aristotle Ontology

Aristotle remarks in his *Metaphysics* that the persistently perplexing question, "What is Being?" is really the query, "What is substance?" (1028B3). The "Being" referenced here is our old friend, *to on* (from the verb *einai*, "to be"), and "substance" translates the Greek *ousia*, a noun formed from the feminine participle of the same verb.[1]

According to Aristotle, *to on* has many meanings, for we can say *it is* in numerous ways—"the man is a professor," "the woman is running," "the cat is on the bed," "the dog is 56 pounds"—but in its primary sense, he says, *being* denotes an individual—*this* man or *this* horse. And he conceptualizes an individual as one enduring entity to which adhere many shifting properties. So, for example, a man endures as an individual despite changes in his health, his height and weight, his dispositions and beliefs; despite his passage through space and time; or his varying relations and relationships to the world and

---

[1] If you wonder whether Aristotle belongs in a history of Platonism, see Lloyd Gerson's *Aristotle and Other Platonists* (Cornell, 2006).

other people. His identity as one and the same particular thing abides throughout a lifetime of qualitative transformations; and any such durably self-sufficient and self-identical individual is a *being* in the fullest sense of the word.

Some of the Roman philosophers later employed the word *substantia*, our "substance," to translate the technical term *ousia*, and the word is appropriate because the individual in a sense "stands under" (*sub-stans*) its properties as a stable ground atop which flit a multiplicity of qualities and relations. The substance is that which stays the same "beneath" or "behind" its changing properties. Think of the relation as a matter of ontological dependence: the properties of a substance depend for their existence on the substance *in which* or *of which* they are said to be. The substance, on the other hand, is ontologically autonomous—its being doesn't depend on its properties: it is simply said *to be*, in and of itself, period. The "grey-haired" depends on the man; the man doesn't depend on the "grey-haired." So, although Aristotle is happy to call both individuals and their properties "beings" (*ta onta*), for him the individual substance is most truly Being. As a philosophical concept in this context, then, "substance" indicates that which is most fully and actually real, the ultimate principle or principles of reality, ontological bedrock.

Aristotle's revision of Plato here is significant. Plato's *ta onta* are Forms, the eternal, immaterial, universal essences of things, existing "beyond the heavens," apart from, but somehow causally related to, the things whose essences they are. The separation of the Forms from the things they enform particularly bothered Aristotle: it made no sense to him that the essence of a thing could be separate from the thing whose essence it is. Hence, whereas for Plato the incorporeal

Form of *human* would be a substance, for Aristotle the substance would be this or that corporeal man.

As significant as was Aristotle's dispute with Plato over the nature of Being, his assent to the master's insight that it's Being that makes reality real and knowledge possible was critical to the trajectory of western thought. He, too, emphatically rejected the Heraclitean doctrine of radical Becoming, which makes of reality a sort of phantasmagoric cloud formation that's perpetually in transition and never what it appears to be—because it isn't really anything at all.

Now, let's just pause to make sure we understand the role of Being (or "substance"—and we may use the words interchangeably now) in ontology and epistemology. In ontology, Being is the really real; in epistemology, it's the truly knowable.[2] If all things are always changing in every way, as Plato expressed Heraclitus' doctrine of Becoming, then nothing is ever the same as itself from one moment to the next—nor even at one and the same moment—which is as good (or bad) as there being no things at all. Nothing is real in any functional sense. And it follows that there aren't any objects of knowledge either: there's nothing there to be known, for as soon as the mind reaches out to grasp a thing, it's gone; it has changed. More, it wasn't there as a self-identical "thing" to begin with. And, if you think about it, that doesn't even really matter, because there are no minds to search for knowledge anyway. There's no more "you" or "I" persisting amid the flux of Becoming than there is anything else, so no "your mind" or "my mind" either; no enduring ego, self, or psyche.

---

[2] In *Republic* Book 5 we learn that "that which completely is is completely knowable" (*to . . . pantelôs on pantelôs gnôston*, 477a).

You see? Universal Becoming admits of neither knowers nor objects of knowledge. Nothing is stable, and nothing is reliable. Think about it this way: Why do we trust an engineer's assurance that a bridge of *these* specifications will dependably carry *this* amount of weight? Why do we believe that acorns, if they grow, will grow into oak trees? What justifies an astronomer's inference from a deviation in the course of a distant star to the local presence of a planet or some other massive object? What's the point of teaching expectant mothers how to care for a newborn baby? All these things assume patterns of regularity in nature: they suppose that steel has consistent weight-bearing properties; that there's a regular relationship between specific types of seeds and trees; that the law of gravity operates uniformly across space and time (with rare and understood exceptions, as immediately after the Big Bang); and that the nutritional needs of the human animal are generally the same no matter the individual.

Are there really such regularities in nature? There certainly seem to be. But how can we be sure? Couldn't it happen that, from tomorrow, newborn humans thrive on a diet of moonlight and fertilizer? Or that acorns sprout and grow to be roosters? That skyscrapers constructed of playdough and plastic are structurally sound? Or that massive objects repel each other, or transform one another into elephants or five-sided triangles?

We expect things of the same kind to function in the same manner across space and time because we assume that kinds have invariant "natures" or "essences" that regulate their behavior. It's the nature of the human animal to require specific types of nourishment; it's the nature of steel to have certain mechanical properties; it's the essence of a triangle to have three sides. The natures of things endure and thereby ensure reliable regularities. And because they're fixed and enduring—solid ground against the rushing river of Becoming—we refer to them in brief as "Being." Different philosophers advocate different accounts of Being—as Plato and Aristotle disagree on this score—but those who believe in the really real and truly knowable will find a place in their system for something somehow permanent and invariant, for something, that is to say, that we may refer to as "Being."

Despite his rejection of Plato's account of Forms—specifically the idea that Forms are separate from things—Aristotle affirmed his own version of the doctrine. Every individual substance (*this* man or *this* horse) is a metaphysical compound of matter and form—and by "metaphysical compound" I mean to suggest that matter and form are fundamental principles of a thing's being; they're not two physical parts that one could distinguish with the eyes or hold in one's hands. The distinction is ontological, not material. This is Aristotle's "hylomorphism," so called from the Greek words for matter (*hylê*) and form (*morphê*). A human is a human, for example, because a particular bundle of matter is enformed by the substantial form of *human*. The form is that which makes the matter to be a human as opposed to an ox or an oak tree. Unlike Plato's Form, however, Aristotle's form doesn't exist apart from the matter it enforms. In the real world, matter is always enformed and form is always embodied. And it's the substantial form that unifies the matter, which in itself is a plurality of disparate elements. It also supplies the substance with its nature—indeed, it *is* its nature, its essence, and as such it's the guarantor of its constancy and its coherence as a unified entity.

What makes a one of many, then? What bonds an individual's several parts into a unified whole while marking it off from its surroundings, even those it interacts with most intimately, on a micro-level? How do I stay the same even as so many of my properties change? What makes you you, a being, and not a mere fluctuation in the field of Becoming? Substantial form. Embodied substantial form, enformed matter, a hylomorphic compound—to say the same thing three ways—is a substance, and a substance is an objectively real, enduring, self-identical individual thing. This man or this horse. And to say it again: substance, Being, regarded ontologically, is the *real*; regarded epistemically, it's the *true*.

11

Aristotle
Ethics

A friend of mine once declared Aristotle's *Nicomachean Ethics* the most correct work ever written. It's hard to disagree, though there may be one or two *as* correct. (It matters that he didn't say "true.") In any case, it's an ideal text to consult for a cogent account of an objectivist ethics. To be sure, Plato's ethics are every bit as objectivist; but Aristotle makes the case more clearly and directly.

Aristotle grounds his account of ethics on Being, on Being as substance, and substance as matter and form—substantial form—specifically the form of *human*. In short, for Aristotle good and bad flow from human nature. His reasoning runs: because *this* is the nature (or essence) of a human, *these* activities are good for a man and *those* are bad. It's equivalent to saying that given the nature of the *Bellis perennis* plant, these daisies will flourish within *this* temperature range with *this* much exposure to sunlight and water, but they'll die with too great an excess or deficiency of any of these factors. A human is more complex than a flower, so the practical details of ethics are more elaborate than those of gardening; but the rationale is identical.

So the first step in determining what's good and bad for a human—or what constitutes *a good human life*—is to get clear about what a human is. What's the nature of a human being? To answer this question, Aristotle asks another question: What's the distinctive activity of a human? What is it about the human animal—what it's like and what it does—that distinguishes it from all other things? The answer to this question reveals those traits without which a man wouldn't be a human—he'd be a thing or an animal, but not a *human* animal—which is to say, those characteristics that are *necessary* for something to be a human, the *necessary properties* of a human, or, in short, the *essence* of a human, *human nature*.

What is it then that sets a human apart from everything else in the universe? It's not, for example, three-dimensionality or temporality, which characterize most everything there is. But most everything isn't alive: the human's a living organism, unlike many other spatio-temporal entities. True, but numerous other things *are* alive, and they aren't humans—flowers, for instance, or stalks of corn—so "life" won't do as the distinctively human trait. How about sensibility then? Flowers and other forms of vegetation lack the faculty of sensation that's so characteristic of human experience. However, the other species of animal share the sensitive powers to some extent, some to an even greater extent than we do. So "sensitive" won't do either. But now consider our rational faculty: no animal besides the human reasons as we are reasoning now. Sure, one can imagine dolphins in their depths proving mathematical theorems, or the chimpanzee with faraway eyes pondering the meaning of life; but despite the intelligence displayed by many other animals, none attains to the level of human rationality.

Hence the traditional rough-and-ready definition of a human as *the rational animal*.

The distinctively human life, then, is the rational life. The person who lives to eat and drink lives the life of a plant; the person who lives for sights and sounds lives an animal's life; only the person who habitually engages in thoughtful, reflective activity lives a specifically *human* life. This is not to say that a human can neglect all other forms of action. Intellect is essential to our being what we are, but we're more than disembodied minds: we're living bodies, sensing beings, and social animals. So, although reason is the highest human faculty, a full human life will include the proper exercise of our many other faculties as well.

Now that we've identified the structural characteristics of a human life, we can pose the crucial question: What makes a *good* human life? Yes, this is the question. We want more than just to live; we aim for the good life. But, if you think about it, the solution's obvious, at least in a general sense: a good human life is a human life *lived well*. What we want to do as humans is to engage in rational activities—also in typically human physical, perceptive, and social activities—and to engage in them *well*. It's pretty much tautological: to do the human things well is to be a good human. The catch is to determine what it is to do these things well. But, actually, there isn't much of a conundrum here, either; this is obvious too, generally speaking anyway. There's a common word for that which enables one to do what one does well: virtue. Let me explain.

When I was a child the word "virtue" conjured spectral impressions of a nebulous mystery or hovering spiritual phantasms; it was a concept studded with ceremonial gems brandished by authorities as a moralizing spook or a cudgel. But that was just my ignorance and naivety. In truth, a virtue is actually quite mundane. Our word "virtue" translates the Greek *aretê*, which means "excellence," an attribute of a thing that enables it to do what it does well. That's it; it's that simple. And a vice would be an attribute that inhibits a thing from functioning well, or that causes it to function poorly. So, for example, solidity is a virtue in a bridge but a vice in a trampoline. Permeability to water is a virtue in grass seed but a vice in raincoats. A long, straight, thin beak is a virtue in a hummingbird but a vice in a hawk.

Now, I've noted already that the human is a complex animal, so we have a wider range and variety of virtues and vices than do trampolines or hummingbirds. But it still comes down to the difference between those attributes or states that enable us to do what we do as humans well and those that frustrate our doing so. For humans as living organisms, a low resting heart rate is a virtue; a high heart rate is a vice. As sensing mammals, 20/20 vision is a virtue; myopia is a vice. As social beings, affability is a virtue; irascibility is a vice. As moral persons, prudence is a virtue, carelessness a vice. And as rational agents, wisdom is a virtue, ignorance a vice.

It's true that the virtues of the human specifically *as an agent* involve knowledge, intentionality, and voluntary behavior, unlike the operational virtues or excellences of the heart or a trampoline, but the kernel of the concept "virtue" is the same in either case: to perform one's essential function well. So the person who knows what's virtuous to do in any particular situation, and who gladly chooses to do it, lives well. And the result is that *the virtuous life is the good life*. But since this isn't a book of practical ethics, we need not pursue these matters in too much more detail. You can (and you should) read the *Nicomachean*

Ethics for yourself for a thorough treatment of the virtues and the good human life. It's worth noting here, though, that, according to Aristotle, such popular pursuits as pleasure, wealth, and honor don't make for a good life in and of themselves. They can enhance a life lived well; but they're no substitute for moral and intellectual virtue. A bad man, however prosperous, esteemed, or gratified he may be, lives a bad life.

It flows quite naturally, doesn't it? What is a good human life? Well, what is a human? And what does it take to live well? A human is an animal that is sensitive, social, and, above all, rational. And to live well is to engage in physical, sensitive, social, and, above all, rational activities according to their proper virtues, which is to say, in accord with those attributes or states that enable a thing to do what it does well. In sum, as Aristotle puts it: the chief good for a human is a life of intellectual activity in accord with virtue.

So the human good follows from human nature. Now mark what this implies: like the *real* and the *true*, the *good* is objective, and its objectivity is grounded on substantial form, which is to say, on Being. And here it is again: *terra firma* in the river of Becoming, Being as solid ground. There's no place for moral objectivity in a world of total flux, the waters of which undermine the foundations of fixed value. Hence, Heraclitus' relativism and Nietzsche's "beyond good and evil." Being and objectivity are twins; the loss of one entails the loss of the other.

I've said that Plato was every bit the objectivist that Aristotle was. He, too, explicitly ties goodness to Being; but to say even just this much (or little) is to gesture toward ideas that extend well beyond the scope of this book. Some are pertinent, though; so I'll elaborate, but only just a little.

In his *Republic* Plato writes of the good in a manner that invites one to capitalize the word. The Good is somehow superior to the other Forms—more, it may be something *other than* a Form. As I mentioned in a previous chapter, Plato refers in Book 6 to "the Idea of the Good"; and although he does sometimes employ the word "Idea" (*idea* in Greek) to refer to Forms (more often the word is *eidos*), he seems in this case to intend to mark a distinction. Indeed, the Idea of the Good, he says, gives to the Forms their intelligibility, their existence (*to einai*), and their essence (*tên ousian*). And then he adds, remarkably, that the Good itself is "beyond essence (*epekeina tês ousias*), exceeding it in dignity and power" (509b). Treatises have been written on these words; I'll confine myself to observing that this notion of "the Good beyond essence" (often translated as "beyond being") recurs throughout the history of western thought, particularly in the context of mysticism, Christian or otherwise. As Plato's Good is the transcendent source of the really real (the Forms), so the mystics' God surpasses his creation so profoundly as to be altogether unknowable: recall that Being, substance, essence is (among its other roles) the object of knowledge. If this is so, then that which really is "beyond essence" must be unintelligible.[1]

But to conclude by returning to Aristotle while keeping the divine in mind: In Book 10 of the *Ethics* Aristotle addresses the place of God in the good human life. The divine is a substance too, less mystically

---

[1] Apart from its influence on western mysticism, the Idea of the Good adds a layer of depth to Plato's moral objectivism that I have not explored here. See Lloyd Gerson's *Plato's Moral Realism* (Cambridge, 2023).

extraordinary than Plato's "Good beyond being," but still a substance greater than any hylomorphic compound (this man or this horse). God as a substance is an immaterial, immortal, purely enduring actuality; and as such God is Being through and through, without the slightest admixture of Becoming, untainted by generation, alteration, or corruption. I should also add—though there's no need here to go into details—that Aristotle's god is a mind or intellect engaged eternally in thinking, and thinking only of the greatest object of thought, namely, itself. Literally, Intellect intellecting Intellect, he calls it. He also calls it the Prime Mover, the unmoving source of all the movement, and therefore all the life, in the universe.

The first principle of all things, "transcendent in blessedness" (1178B), Aristotle's God is the highest possible object of knowledge and desire. Aquinas will later compress these thoughts into a concise summary: The highest human life engages the highest human faculty with its highest object. The highest human faculty is the intellect, and the intellect's highest object is the divine. Therefore, the highest human life—the *good* life, indeed *the best life*—is the life of one who engages habitually in the contemplation of God.

Thus do the pinnacle of philosophy and the end of a distinctly human life coincide in the unification of knower and known, lover and beloved: The "I" in communion with Being.

12

Plotinus

Half a millennium separates Plotinus from his master, Plato; but he writes as if as a young student he'd sat at the sage's feet. He regards himself a loyal disciple, a Platonist through and through; and, indeed, for two thousand years most everyone accepted his self-assessment—until, in the nineteenth century, scholars dubbed his thought "Neo-Platonism." It's true (maybe, but—given Plato's intentional obscurity—who can really say?) that there's much in Plotinus' work that Plato likely never dreamed of, for the Platonism he inherited descended from thinkers who formulated the abstruse doctrines of so-called "Middle-Platonism." And while there's no need now to go into a history of that tradition,[1] be aware that Plotinus' brand of Platonism is an eclectic fusion of ideas.

At the center of Plotinus' philosophy is the notion that the whole of physical reality is contingent on a threefold source of eternal, immaterial, transcendent principles, which Plotinus calls "hypostases." The word in Greek (*hypostasis* is the singular form) is identical in its literal meaning to the Latin *substantia*: the "hypo"

---

[1] See John Dillon's *The Middle Platonists* (Cornell, 1996).

means "under" and the "stasis," from the verb *histêmi*, "to stand." A hypostasis, then, is that which "stands under" in the sense of being a foundation of the real; it's ontologically fundamental. These three principles, or substances, from which the cosmos descends, and back to which all things strain to return, stand to one another in a hierarchy of dependence. The lesser of the three, the World Soul, is generated by the Intellect, which in its turn is issue of the supreme substance, the One. Solitary and singular, self-contained and self-sufficient, the One is the first, the primordial, the originary principle of all things, finite or infinite, eternal or temporal.

It's impossible to explain in brief the process whereby the One generates the Intellect. Let's just say that the One is engaged eternally in something like self-contemplation,[2] through which it enjoys an intellectual vision of itself. And this self-reflective movement is productive of being: the One's vision of itself produces—or really it just *is*—a second structural feature of reality, a new substance, the Intellect. This second hypostasis, being an offspring of the One, and therefore its ontological inferior, is not a pure unity but rather a multiplicity. This "many-ness" of the Intellect is all that distinguishes it from the One. It's as though the One, a singular entity viewing itself in a multifaceted mirror, sees its likeness reflected as a multiplicity of varied images, and this manifold-reflection, this new reality, is the Intellect and its thoughts—and each of these thoughts is a Form. Yes, a Form: Plotinus conceives Plato's Forms as ideas in the hypostatic Intellect.

---

[2] But don't take this literally because none of our words or concepts actually apply to the One.

The Intellect too engages in something like self-contemplation, and, as before, this reflective activity is productive of new being, in this case the third hypostasis, the World Soul. And here there's yet another addition of many-ness. If the Intellect is the One's singular vision of itself as a multiplicity, the World Soul is the Intellect's multiple vision of itself as a compound-multiplicity. Whereas the One in reflecting on itself sees the Forms of, say, *triangle*, *beauty*, and *human*, the Intellect in reflecting on itself as these Forms sees the many triangles, things of beauty, and human beings that populate material reality. It's as though the Intellect, a multiplicity viewing itself in a multifaceted mirror, sees its likeness reflected as a multitude of multiplicities of varied images—and this multi-manifold-reflection, this new reality, is the World Soul and all the many individual souls through which it knows each simplex immaterial Form as a plurality of material things.

This process whereby the second hypostasis descends from the first, and the third from the second, Plotinus refers to as "emanation." He likens the One to an eternal fountain endlessly overflowing, its run-off generating, or just being, the first and second hypostases; or to the sun radiating light with no depletion of its energy, its rays generating, or just being, the other hypostases. The place of matter in this system is debated. The material cosmos, the world as we experience it through our senses, is either a manifestation of the outermost tide of the fountain's overflow, the farthest reach of the sun's dissipating light, or else it's just beyond these limits, on the far side of the real, adrift in the void of nothingness, as it were. In any case, the point is that matter is only just barely, if even at all, progeny of the One; and for reason of this remoteness, this alienation even, it's the principle of imperfection, error, and evil.

Here we have an instance of so-called "*Phaedo*-Platonism," a tendency in Plato and some Platonists to disparage matter and the body in contrast to the incorporeal soul and the Forms, a tendency manifest most fully in Plato's *Phaedo*, a dialogue set on the day of Socrates' death. Philosophy itself is identified there as a practice involving the separation of the soul from the body, which is death, but which, affected to the extent possible while alive, is "purification." Only the pure soul can know truth and be good. So influenced was Plotinus by this idea that his student Porphyry reported that he seemed ashamed to be in a body. We've just seen that he regards matter as the source of all that's erroneous and bad; and for him it follows that matter is also responsible for ugliness. Hence his insistence that, quite apart from the labor of approaching the *true* and the *good*, to attain to the *beautiful* the philosopher must undergo a spiritual, intellectual, and moral purification; only thus can one commune as pure soul with pure Being.

Since Plotinus takes the Forms to reside in Intellect, he refers to the second hypostasis as Being. It's the realm of *ta onta*, the essences; it's the realm of the really real. And in what may be today his most famous treatise, he attributes beauty to the influence of this hypostasis. What's the source of beauty, he wonders, the beauty of sights, of sounds, even of souls and ways of life? Diversity gathered into unity by the imposition of form. Matter of itself is diverse and disordered, the source of all that's irrational and unattractive. Form provides a channel through which the One cascades from its heights into our dimension, carrying with it order and reason, the loveliness of harmony.

In this Plotinus echoes Plato, who in his *Symposium* treats the Form of *beauty* as a sort of stand-in for the ultimate principle. The lover of wisdom, he says, will pursue beauty up the rungs of what's come to be called "the ladder of love," ascending from the erotic desire for an individual beautiful body to the love of the human form in general; from there to the love of souls and the customs and laws that make souls beauteous; thence to the love of learning and knowledge; and, finally, to the love of Beauty Itself, which "always is, neither comes to be nor passes away," which is "itself according to itself," "pure," and not corrupted by "human flesh and coloring and so much mortal nonsense besides" (211a–e). So the final object of the philosopher's desire, at the apex of the hierarchy of love, is Being.

Today we're raised on the modern, anti-Platonic platitude that "beauty's in the eye of the beholder." Hence, we tend to be aesthetic subjectivists: "beauty" is whatever anyone happens to find attractive. The pre-modern tradition held that beauty is an objective property grounded on Being. Like the *true* and the *good*, the *beautiful* is what it is independent of our sentiments or perceptions. Beauty *is*; it's really real; it's an actually existing entity: *to on*.

Like his master Plato, then, Plotinus is a consummate objectivist. But at the same time he's a mystic. Considered by many the father of western mysticism, Plotinus applies Plato's expression "beyond being" to the One. And why not? The One is after all the transcendent source of the second hypostasis, which he calls "Being." So, for as much as he writes about the One, it is finally ineffable. Plato's Good is the source of the Forms; Aristotle's God is an immaterial intellect eternally contemplating itself, and it's the first cause of motion in the universe. Plotinus unites these twin conceptions of God as the Good and God as the Source in his first hypostasis, the One, which he's happy to call "God" and even "Father." As the singular, simple, timeless source of all things, Plotinus' One is the archetype with reference to which many later thinkers will fashion their image of the divine. As we shall see.

Now, imagine a sphere, a radiant sphere, a sphere so incandescent it's all but unimaginable, as if it were luminosity incarnate. Imagine its magnitude so great that every point on its surface is infinitely distant from every other, but so pure the simplicity of its unity that as a whole it's but a partless point; an infinite volume with a diameter of zero. Imagine its aura so dynamically potent as to be fecund, so generative of being that around it forms another sphere fashioned from the brilliance of its beauty. Imagine the surface of this second sphere an array of images, each figure constituted as its own unique self by mirroring all the others at a single focal point. Now imagine yet a third sphere gleamingly reflecting around the second, a kaleidoscopic projection of the second's images, its outermost surface (or the abysmal void just beyond its rim) abuzz with activity and movement, as though all the figures of the second sphere were there multiplied and vivified as an infinitely varied animated environment, a world entire. Imagine these three nested spheres each at a measureless distance from each and each interpenetrating all. See the central fiery furnace perpetually burning, radiating, discharging its inexhaustible core into and as the circumambient atmosphere, generating being and life in an effusion of riches that never diminishes but ever proliferates as an endless expansion of reality. Imagine all this and still you haven't adequately envisioned Plotinus' conception of our cosmos and the three principal hypostases on which it hangs.

13

Sextus Empiricus

Pyrrho of Elis accompanied the army of Alexander the Great into India. He wrote nothing himself, but some insist that the accounts of his ideas recorded by his friend Timon are the earliest evidence we have (not just in the West but anywhere) for the teachings of Gautama the Buddha. Timon reports that Pyrrho held that things in themselves are undifferentiated by logical distinctions, unstable, and therefore undecidable, and that as a consequence our perceptions and opinions are unreliable. From this he took it to follow that the sage should not commit to beliefs about reality that aren't obvious or evident. This attitude of detachment, he said, will engender a state of *ataraxia*, inner peace or, literally, "undisturbedness." The Buddha famously taught that all things are empty of self-nature, impermanent, and unsatisfactory; he refused to take a position on non-evident metaphysical matters beyond this; and he maintained that by abandoning attachments to external things one can attain the peace of enlightenment.[1]

The parallels are remarkable, but as we have so little reliable information about Pyrrho himself, we must study instead the

---

[1] See Christopher Beckwith's *Greek Buddha* (Princeton, 2015).

tradition named for him, Pyrrhonism, or Pyrrhonian skepticism. Our best source for this school is the work of Sextus Empiricus, a medical doctor living a century or so before Plotinus (his dates are uncertain).[2] He authored several books on Pyrrhonian skepticism, many of which have come down to us, the most useful of the lot for our purposes being the *Outlines of Pyrrhonism*.

Sextus begins this text by distinguishing the Pyrrhonians' brand of skepticism from both "dogmatic" philosophy—such as the system of Aristotle—and "Academic" philosophy, named for Plato's Academy, which a few generations after the master's death was dominated by a skepticism of a different variety. The Academic skeptics were, let's say, negative dogmatists: they insisted that knowledge is impossible, and that they could demonstrate the fact. The Pyrrhonians for their part affirm only that it seems to them that they lack knowledge, but still they claim to desire it, and so they continue to search for it. Their philosophy is, Sextus says, *zetetic*, which is to say, investigative, inquiring, always seeking.

In practice though this hardly seems sincere. At the heart of Pyrrhonism are collections of various so-called "modes," which are observations and arguments designed to establish that, respecting any particular truth-claim, the contrary is equally plausible, and that therefore no determination as to the truth of either claim is possible. As a consequence of this, the Pyrrhonians advised, one should decline to commit to either side of the dispute; and this state of suspended judgment due to the equipollence of contrary ideas, they referred to

---

[2] I put Sextus after Plotinus to position skepticism as close as reasonably possible to the Moderns, for whom epistemology was an urgent concern, much more so than it was for Plato, Aristotle, and Plotinus.

as *epochê*. The modes function, then, as arrows in the skeptic's quiver to launch against any imposing wind-bag of a philosopher's claim to knowledge: they're weapons of intellectual war the Pyrrhonian deploys to annihilate every ordinance in the enemy's armory. Thus equipped, he need never commit to an assertion or denial that presumes to pronounce on any matter beyond the immediately apparent. Confronted with any such declaration, he draws back his bow, lets fly an arrow, and says, "I don't know." Then he turns and walks away.

The idea is that by thus refusing to commit oneself to either side of a debate, one's mind will rest at ease. No more the stress of vacillating between approval and dissent; no more worrying over the soundness of convoluted arguments; no more second-guessing one's own premises and inferences, suspicious even of one's own mind. As the sea after a turbulent storm finally settles and rolls easy, so the philosopher after contentious years defending and refuting controversial ideas can at last relax and rest content with what's apparent, letting every other obscure matter, or curious character, go its own way. This is the state of undisturbed tranquility—as manifest in a calm sea or a serene philosopher—that the Greeks called *ataraxia*.

For all their desire for peace and quiet, though, the skeptics stirred up endless trouble, not only among their peers but for centuries afterward. Their arguments and ideas are relevant to this day, but they're much less directly influential than they were among the Ancients and, for a time, the early Moderns. Still, it's worth at least acquainting ourselves with their philosophy, the modes in particular, not only for historical reasons but because their vision is fascinating, and, to some, positively alluring.

I have said that there are collections—plural—of modes, and, indeed, Sextus includes in his *Outlines* accounts of the "ten modes of Aenesidemus," the "five modes of Agrippa," the "two modes," and the "eight modes," the latter two collections of uncertain origin. The ten include, for example—and these are the first three—modes depending on differences among animals, differences among humans, and conflicts among the sense organs. So, because a fly presumably sees the world quite differently than we do (considering especially the structure of its eyes), and is attracted to things that disgust us; or since there's no consensus in human perception and judgment of the world; or since what appears red to the eye appears smooth to the touch and hollow to the ear: because of all such discrepancies and disagreements, and there being no neutral vantage point from which to decide among them, there's no way to know which assessment or observation is correct. Therefore, one should suspend one's judgment about the true nature of things themselves.

But is there really no way to adjudicate such controversies? This question generates the so-called "problem of the criterion": who, or what, is the arbiter of truth? Suppose someone insists that only sensory information is reliable. To what standard or criterion might he appeal to justify the claim? To be consistent he'd have to say it's justified by sense experience, but this just isn't so—there's no empirical fact to which we can point that attests that only sense experiences are true—and, besides, it begs the question at issue. Nor could he say that reason confirms it, because it doesn't, and especially because his very claim is that only sense experience is confirmatory—so what good would any ostensible "confirmation by reason" do?

There's a variation on this presentation of the problem of the criterion that's sometimes called "Agrippa's trilemma." The skeptics won't admit that truth can be established by mere assertion: there are no properly "basic" truths (this is the fourth of the "five modes of Agrippa"). Therefore, any proposed truth-claim will have to be justified by argument. But an argument must either (a) finally depend on some purportedly "basic" truth that needs no further proof, which, as we've just seen, is unacceptable; or else it must (b) proceed to justify it's every justification ad infinitum, but no infinite sequence of inferences can finally ground a proposition (this is the second of the "five modes"); or (c) at some point in the inferential chain an assertion will depend for its justification on an earlier assertion that it itself is meant to play a part in justifying, but this is circular logic—x is true because y, and y is true because x—and such reasoning is invalid (this is the fifth of the "five modes"). Therefore, since no non-evident assertion can be justified either as basic or as inferentially grounded, no such assertion can be justified at all.

Pyrrhonian skepticism quite obviously undermines philosophical objectivism, or at least the confident commitment thereto. It may well be that *reality, truth, goodness,* and *beauty* exist and are what they are independently of human thought, but there's no way to know for sure. Assertions of moral or aesthetic objectivity affirm as fact propositions whose content reaches beyond the immediately apparent. It's evident that people and cultures entertain different ideas about these matters, and that each boasts to have truth on its side; but who really is right, and whether there is a fact of the matter distinct from the disputants' conflicting opinions—this the Pyrrhonian argues cannot be determined. Were such a view to take hold in a population, whether or not there were objective truth, the people wouldn't believe in it; and for practical purposes in many cases, if not in all, this would amount to their actively disbelieving it.[3]

In the turmoil of the grisly collapse of the Western Roman Empire, Sextus' works were lost (as were so many others, alas) and eventually forgotten. But as they were recovered, translated into Latin, and more and more widely diffused during the fifteenth and sixteenth centuries, they became quite influential, especially among philosophers in France. Thus, famously, Michel de Montaigne infused his popular *Essays* with the spirit of Pyrrhonism, thereby injecting skepticism into the intellectual bloodstream of modern Europe. And although it's unknown whether Descartes read Sextus directly, he was no doubt familiar with Pyrrhonian arguments, not only by way of Montaigne but through his friend and regular correspondent Marin Mersenne. In any case, the contemporary revival of skepticism, and the need in the name of the "new science" to refute it, was a principal motivation behind Descartes' *Meditations*. For we can't know that modern physics is superior to Aristotelian physics if we can't know anything at all.

But let's not get ahead of ourselves. Before adverting to the Moderns—whose novel aspirations, assumptions, and theoretical perspectives upturned the intellectual world in which Platonism made sense—we should trace the development of Platonic thought through some relevant thinkers of the Middle Ages.

---

[3] The attentive reader will have noticed that my account of Pyrrho himself on the first page of this chapter suggests that his is an ontological assertion—the things themselves are indeterminate—whereas Sextus' worry is epistemic, the problem for him being human cognition or reason. According to some scholars, Pyrrho (unlike Sextus) thought he knew something about reality itself, namely that it's indefinite. On either account, we have no access to stable *truth*, *goodness*, or *beauty*, to Being of any sort—because there's no such thing (Pyrrho), or because, even if there is, we can't know it (Sextus).

14

Augustine

I first read excerpts from Augustine's *Confessions* as an undergraduate Philosophy major. I did not enjoy it. I didn't get it. So he stole a few pears from a neighbor's field—did that really warrant such overwrought guilt? Typical morbid Christian self-contempt. Pathetic! Or so I thought. But when many years later I read the whole work through, and I comprehended something of the man's intentions, the true object of his concern and the depth of his self-analysis, then I came to appreciate his spiritual achievement, as a writer and as a human. Augustine was a mystery to himself (as are we all), a labyrinth of self-concealments; and he reflected on his life in words to illuminate the caverns of his psyche that he might find his way through his own profundities to the cloudless heights of God.

Augustine was born and raised in north Africa. His mother, Monica, was a devout Christian, but his father remained a pagan until just before he died; and Augustine himself as a young man was more smitten by rhetoric than he was earnest about religion. He craved worldly success. Among his peers he was recognized as charismatic, brilliant, and supremely well-educated in eloquence and the art of declamation; he was also something of a free-spirit, not to say a rake.

Coming of age, he took a concubine with whom he lived for many years, and together they raised a son (who died as a teenager). The family relocated to Italy when Augustine was twenty-nine, first to Rome and then to Milan, where he achieved success as a teacher of rhetoric. He had many friends, some of whom had followed him from Africa; his beloved mother came too. He even enjoyed relations with the Imperial court. All these riches Augustine had and more—but he was not happy.

At nineteen he had read Cicero's *Hortensius*, which inspired in him a desire for wisdom. The philosophical pursuit of truth seemed the way to happiness, for happiness, he reasoned, attends the acquisition of the object of one's desire—assuming, of course, that one desires the right things—and what object is more desirable than truth? None, actually, because truth is identical to God, or so Augustine came to believe during the period of his conversion to Christianity in Milan, which was prompted by his reading of certain "books of the Platonists" and the influence of the local bishop, Ambrose. But herein lies a complication: if happiness is conditional on obtaining the object of one's desire, and the object in this case is the God who transcends our world, then it's unlikely one will be happy in this life.

In the chapter on Aristotle's ethics, we reviewed the ancient Platonists' account of the good human life. A substantive matter I omitted there—a subject we mustn't overlook, which is why I introduce it here—is the ancient notion of "happiness." I put the word in quotation marks because the Greek word for which this is the standard (mis-)translation signifies a condition contrary to that which we commonly mean by "happiness." The Greek word is *eudaimonia*, which means, quite literally, to be well (*eu*) situated with respect to one's *daimôn*, which is to say one's guiding or guardian spirit. But in this context it's best not to be so literal. Figuratively, one's *daimôn* is the course of one's life, the overall trajectory, circumstances, and character of one's existence. In this sense, one's *daimôn* is, in a word, one's *life*; and to be well situated with respect to it is *to live a good life*. Moreover, and as we've seen, the "good" in this formulation is to be understood as objective: it's not what you or I, our culture, our country, or our age *opines* to be good; it's what *really is* good measured against the standard of human nature.

Today, when we use the words "happy" or "happiness," we mean just about the opposite of what the ancient ethicists intended. Whereas by *eudaimonia* they meant an objective state of being, we tend to mean by "happiness" a subjective state of mind. Winning the lottery, swimming with sharks, or public adoration may make one "happy," if you like that sort of thing; but none of this amounts to a good life. When reading the Ancients in translation, then, one must be careful to understand "happiness" as *eudaimonia*; otherwise much of what they say will make no sense.

Augustine wrote in Latin, so of course he didn't use the word *eudaimonia*. The "happiness" he sought is *beatitudo*, often translated as "blessedness," and it's more or less equivalent in sense to the Greek term. Indeed, Augustine is often labeled a "eudaimonist" because his treatment of "happiness"—both the character of the state itself and the way to achieve it—parallels the structure of the Greek accounts, though with notable variances following from his Christian faith. In particular, as I have intimated, true beatitude comes only after death, and, ultimately, it's a gift from God rather than a state one secures for oneself.

So, despite the structural similarities between Aristotle's and Augustine's modes of reasoning, Augustine's beatitude stands to *eudaimonia* somewhat as *eudaimonia* stands to our "happiness." That's an exaggeration, but it captures an important truth. Being a subjective state of mind, happiness is transitory—we can be "happy" one moment and "unhappy" or "sad" the next. Not so with *eudaimonia*, which characterizes an entire life, within which come and go many fleeting episodes of "happiness" and "sadness." But now consider beatitude: this is a condition of *eternal* life, in comparison to which the natural lifespan of a human is itself but transitory.

Augustine's treatment of happiness, then, centers on God, the supreme principle of reality, the highest object of knowledge and love. He adopts the Platonic vision of an ontologically ordered universe: from the lowest low of nothingness to inorganic matter, from there to animated vegetable life, animal life, and human personhood, upward then to angelic beings and thence to the divine actuality of God. There is a hierarchy of reality and value, and human happiness depends on our aligning our beliefs and desires with the objectively true and good. We should love animals more than plants, for example, and human persons more than animals, and God above all. This is the *ordo amoris*, the "order of love"; and whatever transitory happiness-as-delight (*felicitas*) we may enjoy in this life—not to mention our prospects for future blessedness—depends on our conforming our desires to the proper order. To love the wrong things, or to love the right things in the wrong way, or to the wrong degree, is to suffer the misery of a bad life.

But to say just one more thing about Augustine's conception of the divine: As a Platonist, Augustine believed in Forms; but as a Christian

Platonist he conceived of them as thoughts in the mind of God. The idea wasn't new with him, but it was a break from the teachings of Plotinus. As we have seen, Plotinus locates the Forms in the second hypostasis, the Intellect, because the One, being pure unity, admits nothing of the plurality implied by a mind thinking many thoughts. Augustine disagrees, though he neglects to investigate the implications of his dissent. He states emphatically that Plato's Forms are ideas (or "reasons," *logoi*) in the divine mind, but he ignores the problematic consequence of there being diversity in the simplex unity of God. As for the rest of his account, though, it follows the Platonists' line: the archetypes of God's creative activity, the divine ideas impart necessary, abiding, universal properties to the contingent, ephemeral, particular things that participate in them. Thus they ground the reality of the natures of things, and thereby the regularity of their activity, and thereby in turn the reliability of our inductive knowledge of them.

Augustine deviated from the Platonists too in ascribing personhood to the deity and in not condemning matter as the source of imperfection and evil. His God is not "beyond being," like Plato's Good and Plotinus' One; he is an intentional and loving creator, and the material world he made is good, though fallen souls can misuse it for corrupt purposes. By thus blending Platonic and Judaic conceptions of the divinity, Augustine wed the so-called "God of the philosophers" (pure unity of Being) with the "God of Abraham, Isaac, and Jacob" (a living, caring, acting personality), and so bequeathed to the West the idea of God with which most of us are familiar.

Finally, we should take note of Augustine's entanglement with skepticism, a doctrine that concerned him—though, importantly, did not consume him—throughout his thinking life. He'd encountered

Academic skepticism in Cicero, who authored many of his best works from this perspective, which he presented quite convincingly as not only plausible but high-minded, noble even. Since none of the views we've surveyed here would have been available to Augustine were he convinced that knowledge is unattainable, he had to demonstrate, at least to his own satisfaction, that skepticism can be refuted. He composed an early dialogue, *Against the Academics*, to work through his objections, and he continued to engage with the skeptics later in life as well. In his dialogue he argues, among other things, that no skeptic can refute a man's claim to know that some fact or other seems to him to be so, including his claim to know that it seems to him that he knows many things. The most famous of his refutations, though, versions of which appear in several of his works, is not to be found in *Against the Academics*. This is his argument that anticipates Descartes' *cogito*: If, as the skeptics insist, I am mistaken (about this or that), then I must exist; and this I cannot doubt. The very fact that "I am wrong" entails that "I am." This I know. Therefore it cannot be that we must suspend our judgment regarding every proposition.

Knowledge is possible, after all; and Augustine will seek it out, by way of both his senses and his intellect. Knowledge of the material world he considered a straightforward matter of our being directly acquainted with our immediate environment through our sense organs. To provide an explanation for our knowledge of incorporeal Forms, though, is more complicated. Suffice it to say for present purposes that, although he can't accept Plato's theory of recollection (depending, as it does, on reincarnation), Augustine develops a comparable theory of "illumination" according to which God presents the essences of things directly to our minds in a sort of intellectual vision parallel to sight. The illuminated mind is directly acquainted with truth, and thus possesses knowledge.

Wisdom, truth, knowledge, and happiness are tightly bound together in Augustine's thinking, so it's imperative that he refute skepticism. Hence the frequency of his return to the problem. But this is not to suggest that he ever really doubted the soundness of his counter-arguments: unlike so many modern philosophers, who, once having stepped into the skeptics' maze, never found their way out, Augustine trusted in God to light his way through.

15

Thomas Aquinas

With Aquinas, the tradition we've been reviewing ascends to its zenith. Plato incorporated the stupefying and, truth be told, stultifying insights of Parmenides and Heraclitus into a unified and functional metaphysics. Aristotle improved Plato's account of Forms, and thereby also the theory of knowledge. Plotinus illuminated principles that are only intimated in Plato's late dialogues, and he implied objections to Aristotle's account of the first principle—the Prime Mover, or God, as an intellect—that, together with his own positive treatment, would stimulate later refinements in our conception of the divine. Augustine took in all of this and gave it a distinctively Christian turn; and he deepened our understanding of what today we'd call anthropology and psychology while simultaneously initiating a tradition of thinking about God in a way that incorporates philosophical as well as religious insights. Then there's Aquinas, whose magnificently sweeping, systematic vision of the Whole embraces and perfects all of these developments and more. Comprehensive, coherent, cogent, and clear, nothing even remotely like his symphonic account of God, man, and the universe would be achieved again, much less would anyone surpass it.¹ Indeed, with the waning of Aquinas' influence, the West began its unhurried but inexorable descent toward the nadir of nihilism.

In the book of Exodus, when Moses asks the name of God, the deity replies, *egô eimi ho ôn*. This is often rendered as, "I am who I am," but this fails to capture the significance of the expression. Each of us could say the same thing: I am who I am, and you are who you are, too. So? There's nothing out of the ordinary in being who one is. Sometimes though we read, "I am who am," and this is better, much better; but still it's not quite accurate. The literal translation would be something like: "I am the am-ing one" or, "I am the is-ing one." Somewhat less literal would be, "I am he who is." Faced with such translations, though, one might wonder: What exactly is God claiming to *be*? What does he mean to say he is when he says he *is*? These questions assume a predicative use of "to be": "I am he who is" would be elliptical for, "I am he who is always" or, "I am he who is God," or some other such predication. Aquinas sees it differently. As he understands the utterance, God means to identify himself as Being Itself.² He is proclaiming: "I am Being." So Aquinas denominates God, "*ipsum esse subsistens*," "being itself subsisting," which is precisely *not* to say that God is "a being," nor even that he is "the supreme being." It's to say rather that God is Being Itself, Being as an entity or substance.

But we can be more specific still. I noted in the chapter on his ontology that Plato's use of *to on* (the biblical *ho ôn* is the same definite

---

¹Some will complain that I disregard Hegel. Yes, I do disregard him—you can blame it on Schopenhauer.
²It's unlikely that Aquinas worked with the text of the Greek Septuagint; but this doesn't change the main point, which an understanding of the Greek helps to clarify.

article and participle, but in the masculine rather than neuter gender) is predicative and therefore designates what something is, or essence. Aquinas' great achievement here is to have conceived in full for the first time in the West a notion of Being as *existence*, which is to say, as that power, or force, or act that posits a thing in actuality; that causes it to be something rather than nothing; that causes a thing to *be*, period. To *exist*. God is Being as Existence, the source not only of motion and the essences of things (as the Ancients understood), but of their very actuality. Indeed, in God essence and existence are identical, whereas in all created beings existence is distinct from, and therefore must be added to, their essence. This explains why classical theists insist that God is the one necessary Being while all the many beings are contingent. The point is that reality itself—Reality as opposed to Nothingness—is utterly dependent on the creative act of God.

As we have seen, for Aristotle a substance is a hylomorphic compound, a union of the metaphysical principles of matter and form. Matter as such isn't anything in particular, therefore we may think of it as the *principle of potentiality*: it can become anything at all—flesh or blood, for instance—if given the relevant form, this form being the *principle of actuality* because it actualizes as this (flesh) or that (blood) the potential of matter to become these things. But now take a heap of matter enformed as flesh and blood: we may regard this as matter (the principle of potentiality) in its turn, for it isn't as yet any particular type of organism. It has the potential to be an ox or a man (or any other species of flesh-and-blood animal), but it doesn't become a man in fact until enformed by the human form (the principle of actuality). In short, the potentiality of matter as flesh-and-blood enformed by the actuality of human nature is a human being.

Or so it is according to Aristotle. But this is where Aquinas' innovation becomes relevant: for Aquinas, this hylomorphic compound of matter-as-potentiality and form-as-actuality, this amalgam of flesh-and-blood and human nature: this substance considered as a unit is itself now but a new potentiality—which Aquinas calls *essence*—in relation to a still higher, or deeper, actuality, namely, *existence*. So: the potentiality of matter as flesh-and-blood plus the actuality of the form of human produces the human essence, which is a new potentiality, namely, a potential human being. When (if) this *essence-as-potentiality* is actualized by the act of existence (*existence-as-actuality*), then (and only then) we have an *actually existing human being*.

Plato, Aristotle, and Plotinus thought the universe eternal; they had no conception of reality itself coming into being. Individual things come to be; not as newly existing entities come to be as posits in reality, but rather as eternally existent matter taking on new form to come to be a new type of thing. The former is the existential sense of "to come to be"—to come to be, period—the latter the predicative sense—to come to be y from having been x. The Ancients of course knew the difference between, say, Socrates alive and Socrates dead, Socrates being and not being—not being here, or anywhere, now. But they hadn't isolated the notion of existence itself to conceptualize as a phenomenon or fact in need of explanation. Aquinas accomplished this, and he did so by conceiving of being-as-existence as an act, as, let's say, an actualizing event that transforms an essence regarded as a *potentially* existing thing into an *actually* existing entity.

God, then, God as such, is the Pure Act of Existence Itself, which, by sharing its inexhaustible substance with individual essences, actualizes their potential and thereby generates new beings. And whence these essences? They're ideas in the divine mind. I mentioned in the previous chapter that Augustine had the thought that Platonic Forms are God's ideas, but that he never addressed the problem this poses for God's unity: How can a deity that's purely and simply One contain a multiplicity of ideas? Doesn't this make of the One a Many? Well, on Aquinas' account, God doesn't literally think many thoughts in a distinct mind, the mind and the thoughts being discrete "parts" of himself. Rather, through a singular, eternal, all-encompassing act of self-contemplation God understands the many different ways in which his being is imitable, as one might see a single item reflected from countless angles in numberless forms in an infinitely faceted mirror. Each of these reflections of God's being, these pointillist perspectives on the divine, is an essence with a potential toward existence, which may or may not be actualized by God. The universe as a whole, then, is one vast image of the divine as seen from many vantage points, each of these points an individualized likeness of God, an entity, as they say, created in God's image.

But let's return now more specifically to the essences of these entities to introduce a concept that goes back to Plato and Aristotle but which so far I haven't mentioned. I have said that an essence provides a thing with its necessary properties such that it behaves or acts regularly, predictably, under all normal circumstances. An acorn (if it grows) will always grow into an oak tree, never a rooster. And this is so because the essence determines the end-state or goal toward which things of particular kinds are oriented, as acorns are oriented toward oak trees, not roosters. The word for this end or goal is *telos*, and "teleology" is the term for the idea that things by nature are oriented toward ends or goals in this way. Now don't be silly: there's no suggestion of intentionality here; no one thinks that acorns consciously strive to become oak trees. The claim is rather about regularity: acorns under normal conditions regularly become oak trees, and we can count on this when making inferences about the natural world as far into the future or past as one cares to project. We don't need to see it happen in every case to be sure of it: we know it happens, has happened, and will happen because it's the nature of acorns to have this teleological orientation, and, as Aristotle says, nature is what happens always or for the most part.

So the Platonist account of reality (and I mean to include Aquinas as a "Platonist" in this sense) is teleological: from the motions of the particulate elements to the behavior of the celestial bodies, all things in the universe track regular patterns of activity, because all things (all actual substances, that is, as opposed to fictional or socially constructed pseudo-things) are enformed by essences. So the Platonist tradition is essentialist too. It's teleological *because* it's essentialist.

From the elements to the celestial bodies: included within this sweep are human beings. A fertilized human egg (if it grows) will grow into a human, not an oak tree or a rooster. And this human will be characterized by various essential properties that regulate its behavior and activities: it will walk, not fly; it will survive on meat, fruits, vegetables, and fresh water, not tree bark and salt water; it will need approximately six to eight hours of sleep every day; its arteries will carry oxygenated blood from the heart into the bloodstream, and its veins will return the blood depleted of oxygen to the heart; etc. These facts about a human's nature determine certain of its values: fresh water is good for drinking; salt water is bad. And here we return to an Aristotelian account of ethics, which we can now modify with Thomist insights. Just as a body to be healthy needs proper nutrition, oxygen, and sleep, so the good life of *eudaimonia* requires such virtues as wisdom, justice, temperance, and courage. The physically unhealthy man may vow he's doing well, but he isn't, as a doctor would tell him if he'd listen. Just so, the ignorant, unjust, self-indulgent coward lives a bad life, whether or not he enjoys it and insists he's doing fine.

Do you see? We humans have natural ends, just as oak trees and roosters do; and we can't evade the consequences. If we drink seawater, we'll get sick. If we slice an artery, we'll die. Similarly, if we're vicious (gluttonous, slothful, promiscuous, impious), although we might (for a while) enjoy happiness-as-delight (pleasure), we won't experience happiness-as-*eudaimonia*; we will not live a good life. And here I'm thinking only of our natural lives in relation to our natural end. But, if Aquinas is right, we humans also have a supernatural end, namely, the beatific vision (similar to Augustine's *beatitudo*). This is knowledge of God's essence unmediated by the body or any distorting modes of cognition; it's the direct apprehension of God through which the souls of the virtuous attain perfect blessedness. This infinite spiritual good is our ultimate *telos*; it follows from the facts of human nature.

These days, for some people, this sort of essentialism is objectionable. They complain that it's restrictive of their freedom; they want to live as they see fit. But, if you think about it, it isn't actually restrictive at all: everyone's at liberty to live as they please. But essentialism does imply that only certain modes of life conform to the human good, only certain ways of living will make one "happy." But that's all right. That's nothing to get angry about; no more than someone remarking that if you toss a ball into the air, it's bound to fall back to earth. You're free to toss it all you like; no one's stopping you. But if you become enraged at the person who notes that it will fall again, or with the fact of its falling—well, then you'll just look foolish, won't you? This insight too goes back to Plato. In the *Gorgias*, Socrates reasons that the man who does what seems good to him to do, if he's ignorant of the good, may well wind up doing what's bad, in which case, although he does what seems good to him, he doesn't do what he wants, because what he wants is to flourish, to live a good life, and that's possible only by doing the good, which he hasn't done. Again, the man might get mad with someone who points this out, as Polus and Callicles get mad at Socrates. But this will no more change the nature of reality (including the reality of human nature and the good human life) than shaking one's fist will prevent a ball tossed in the air from falling back to earth.

Composing his own variation on his predecessors' cosmic theme, Aquinas conceives the universe as a rationally ordered whole, a hierarchy of reality and value extending from base matter at the abysm beneath all structure and form to God himself as the fullness of Being, the architect of the whole, at, and as, the summit—out of reach, out of sight, beyond comprehension even, though accessible in a way through analogy with the supreme element of his creation, the rational soul. God's essence so permeates the whole, infusing all things, that to the extent they participate in his being, these things are real, true, good, and beautiful—because God himself is reality, truth, goodness, and beauty. Unlike all other things, of which these properties are but attributes, God himself is identical to these "transcendentals" (so called because they transcend all categories and apply to everything that is): the *real* is God as the act of existence; the *true* is God as known; the *good*, God as desired; and the *beautiful* is God as admired.

So everything has its place in the divine order, including us. And if we hope to be blessed with good lives, we'll have to conform ourselves to the design specifications inscribed in our essences, which in this case means that we should strive to respect the real, believe the true, desire the good, and admire the beautiful. We should, in short, love God. We need this like an oak tree needs sunshine and water; it's in our nature. As I remarked above: the system is teleological because it's essentialist.

Ah, but you wonder: What if there are no essences? Yes, well: that's a serious matter. And it's the thought that there are no essences, no natures of things—and therefore no teleology nor any measure of the *real*, the *true*, the *good*, and the *beautiful* apart from human subjectivity—this thought is the womb in which modernity foully gestated, an obscene fetus, a monstrous birth, an organism evolving, maturing, creeping inevitably toward its gloomy *telos*, nihilism.

16

William of Ockham

These days, most everyone has heard of "Ockham's razor," the methodological principle advising against multiplying entities beyond necessity. That is to say, when attempting to explain a heretofore unknown phenomenon, one should appeal to no more things or forces than strictly required to account for the facts under investigation. So, for example, if your car won't start and the fuel tank's empty, the lack of gasoline is all one needs to explain its not starting, so one shouldn't speculate about, say, voodoo curses or demonic possession.

Also known as the principle of parsimony, Ockham's razor is, as I noted just above, a methodological suggestion. It's an aid to theory construction; it's not a key that turns the lock on metaphysical truth. To count on the principle uncritically to pump out veridical representations of reality—as many do—is to assume without evidence that reality is always and everywhere ontologically simple. But, lacking an independent demonstration that reality in itself is parsimonious in a manner convenient for human cognition and practical activity—without knowing for certain whether the structure of reality conforms to our most expedient modes of theorizing, we can't trust the razor to carve reality at the joints. Your car might be out of gas *and* have a dead battery. Or, still worse, it might be out of gas, have a dead battery, *and* be cursed. The history of science is punctuated with episodes of the simplest explanation turning out to be incorrect. Moreover—and this is the deeper point—those explanations we consider "correct" because, say, they generate more and better predictions or facilitate the expansion or application of a theory—even their correctness is no indication that they're true in the sense of corresponding to reality. False theories can, and do, work: we send satellites into orbit using equations derived from Newton's account of gravity!

In any case, the subject of this chapter isn't "Ockham's razor" but rather nominalism, which is to say the denial of universals, which can be, but need not be, generated by the deft application of Billy's blade. In the Middle Ages philosophers and theologians commonly referred to what we've been calling essences, forms, and natures as "universals," because (supposedly) they supply the properties that characterize all individuals of a particular kind—all of them, universally. So, for example, rationality is a universal property of humans, as is three-sidedness of triangles. We've seen that for Plato eternal immaterial Forms function as universals, and also that he takes them to exist apart from the individuals whose essences they are. We've seen too that Aristotle, while admitting the reality of forms, argued contrary to Plato that they're not independently existing abstract objects; they're always embodied. This and other sorts of disagreement about the ontological status of forms, or essences, the Medievals put under the heading "the problem of universals."

In this dispute Aquinas espoused a position known today as "moderate realism," which is to say, he denied the fully realist position of Plato—Forms exist in and of themselves separately from the things they enform—but he also rejected the contrary idea that essences are mental or linguistic constructs that we fabricate for ourselves by generalizing from our observations. Essences, he thought, are real features—actual metaphysical principles—of substances in the world; they exist independently of our minds, but (as Aristotle taught) they're always embodied in particulars.

The radical opposite of Platonic realism is nominalism, to which I alluded just above as the contrary position to Platonism also rejected by Aquinas. Nominalism is, in short, the denial of universals altogether. For the nominalist, there are no forms, essences, or common natures in things themselves—much less somewhere "beyond the heavens"— but only in our minds or vocabularies, as general concepts or generic nouns. There's the idea of *human*, or of *triangle*, by which we can think of any individual human or triangle, or, imaginatively, all of them as a collection; and there are the words "human" and "triangle" that signify these concepts. Such words and concepts enable us to think and speak about many individuals at once, to group things together in our minds and reason about them in syllogisms. But these words and concepts are "universal" only in the mode of their application: they aren't themselves universal—a concept or a word is just a singular individual—nor do they designate any universal entity outside of the mind. There's no mind-independent abstract *human* or *triangle* to which these words and concepts correspond, not even as embodied in particular things.

Given that we're dealing with medieval intellectuals, it won't surprise you to learn that the problem of universals was bound up with theological speculation. Aquinas stressed the intellectual aspect of God, and, therefore, the rational order embedded in his creation. The cosmos manifests the logic of divine design through regular and harmonious patterns of activity; eternal and unchanging essences are the grooves in which the patterns run. This view of God and nature is commonly known as "intellectualism." William of Ockham adopted the contrary position known as "voluntarism," which derives from *voluntas*, the Latin word for "will."[1] Ockham stresses God's *freedom* and *power*. To his way of thinking, intellectualism places unacceptable restrictions on God's range of activity. To affirm that triangles must have three sides or that acorns (if they grow) will always grow into oak trees is to deny that God could make these things be or act otherwise if he saw fit to do so. But if God really can alter the operations of nature on a whim; if God does indeed enjoy such liberty and potency, then it can't be that the operations of nature are regulated by necessary principles such as essences or forms. Necessity implies permanent invariance; but omnipotent God is sovereign over permanence and impermanence, changelessness and change. Hence, there are no necessities in nature. This is nominalism.

Now notice what follows from this denial of essences, and hence of necessities in nature. Since we can never be sure that nature will behave according to patterns similar to those we've previously observed, we can't make inductive inferences from past to future events—or, well, we can infer all we like, but with much less confidence than is afforded to the intellectualist. The voluntarist-nominalist must monitor events to confirm what's happened, to verify whether his expectations were met. One might suppose that some months after restocking a forest by

---

[1] And here the West takes a turn that will lead, eventually, to Nietzsche.

planting one thousand acorns, one would need to return to confirm that they're growing. The nominalist, though, technically, must confirm not only *that* they're growing but also that *what's* growing are indeed oak trees, not roosters. Rational inference from the nature of oak trees will not suffice, because there are no natures from which to infer. Therefore, the nominalist will have to observe. In this way, nominalism generates empiricism, the view that all knowledge comes only from experience.

And now notice what follows in turn from empiricism. What do we find when we inspect nature with our senses? We find singular individual objects, this or that thing situated here or there at one time or another. In short, we find spatio-temporal physical objects, which is to say, material particulars. We never encounter immaterial universals, nor general things of any kind. The world outside our minds, as far anyway as our senses reveal it to us, is in and of itself composed solely of individual material things. Thus does empiricism tend to generate materialism.[2]

Socrates in Plato's *Phaedo* suggests that empiricism and materialism are intellectually and morally ignoble. To believe that "truth is what the body says it is," he insists, corrupts the soul and debases the body, and the man misled by such opinions is unworthy of philosophy (82d–84b). Empiricism rules out essences; but without essences there can be no objective goodness; and without objective goodness there can be no good life, much less any knowledge of it. The whole must

---

[2]Transferred to the social-political sphere, these developments generate modern individualism and, thence, liberalism. Thomas Hobbes (1588–1679) and John Locke (1632–1704) are relevant here, particularly as advocates of nominalism, empiricism, and materialism (Locke was at least a "weak materialist").

hang together, as we've seen throughout this survey: reality, truth, goodness, and beauty are interwoven with one another, threaded into and through the fabric of the universe. If there are no natural kinds, no commonalities between and among things by which to gather them into species and genera, nor any shared, innate, and abiding features characteristic of the different types, then what there is and what we can know is subject to the unfathomable caprice of God, and even morality becomes principally a matter of "divine command"—good and bad determined solely by God's prescriptions and prohibitions. And if God's will is inaccessible to us, or if there just isn't any God: well, then "ontology" and "epistemology" are mere synonyms for *fiction* or *chaos*, and morality is relative or subjective. Everything is up for grabs, metaphysical anarchy.

Nominalism, the denial of universals—the rejection of forms, essences, or natures, call them what you will—amounts in the end to the denial of Being. There may be Being as God; and God may think his thoughts eternally; he may even model our world on his divine ideas. But if we have no communion with him, and if he hasn't embedded his designs in nature in a form to which we have access, then Being is beyond our reach, and God is as good as dead.

17

Descartes

Pity the friendless Frenchman, poor Descartes, subject to such abuse; the scorn of centuries heaped on his head by intellectual malcontents nursing their grievances against modernity; the symbol of European hyper-rationalism; the mind most responsible for severing the best of man from himself, his heart from his head; demeaner of animals, too! "I think, therefore I am," he wrote. Many are those who wish he'd never cogitated, and so never been at all, or at least never written.

With Descartes the West becomes modern by turning dangerously inward—we crawled inside our own heads, got lost in the wilds of subjectivity, and have yet to find the trail leading out of our minds. See for yourself: wander around; have a look. What do you find? Ideas, ideas, and more ideas. Mental images offered up as "representations," but representations of what? We can't say; the images stand in the way of our knowing, looming obstructions between ourselves and the objects of knowledge we seek: things, out there; the external world. And they've been misnamed, these so-called "representations," deceitful damned dissemblers. Step out from behind these painted signs, try to look beyond them, to behold their originals, the "presentations" themselves—and there appear still more images, surrounded in their turn by others large and small, near and far. It's an endless forest of figures—a wooded hall of mirrors—with no pathway into a sunlit clearing.

The Ancients named this wood "Epistemology," and they tended the grounds meticulously. Never overgrown, the district around was a pleasant park, a grove laid out for exercise and reflection. Deep thinking beneath dark foliage, with the occasional frisson of losing one's way, but no need to panic: outlets and egresses were clearly marked. You might have to walk a while; but most everyone found their way out again, striding into the surrounding meadows. These spreading fields they called "Ontology." Waving with the wind, the flowers and grasses bowed in flowing patterns streaming with the breeze; but ultimately the whole was comprehensible by the patient observer, the flora subject to cataloging, sortable by names.[1]

What there is. Ontology. The listing of the items of the real. Yes, that's the matter at hand. It's perplexing but it's manageable; or anyway it once was, long ago. Plato understood that we might be dreaming, but this didn't stifle his thinking; it wasn't for him a reason to doubt the functions of his mind. Indubitable certainty wasn't his goal, nor decisive refutations of every possible counter-thought. But then the Moderns took the subjective turn and lost their way, and the woodland of worry grew wild with uncertainty and doubt. Its range expanded, density thickened, and from that day to this it has entangled most every intrepid spirit who's dared step foot inside.

---

[1] As a matter of historical fact, the words "epistemology" and "ontology" are modern coinages—a note for captious pedants.

Descartes, for one. He entered the thickets with the bold intention to dull the thorns of skepticism once and for all. To this end he inscribed in his first *Meditation* the most thorough set of skeptical arguments he could assemble, from the fact that our senses sometimes mislead us about simple, straightforward perceptions to the possibility of an "evil demon" intentionally deceiving us about mathematical truths and the principles of logic. Then he asked: Confronted with such scenarios, can we be confident that anyone knows anything at all? He finds his answer in the famous *cogito*: "I think, therefore I am." If my senses mislead me about there being a tree in front of me now; if an evil demon convinces me that two and two make three; even if such skeptical possibilities are realized, and I'm mistaken about so much, still I know at least one thing—I know that I exist. To be mistaken is to think incorrectly, but it is at least to think. And if I'm thinking, I must exist. Therefore, even the most radically skeptical arguments fail to undermine knowledge altogether. At least one claim to knowledge—"I am, I exist"—withstands the challenge.

From this granule of certainty Descartes constructs a series of proofs that he knows much else besides, from the existence of God to the reality of the external world. We need not rehearse the details here; suffice it to say that his arguments have not been well received. So, having shut us up inside our minds, hidden from the world behind a tangle of ideas, there Descartes abandoned us, lonely seekers divided within and isolated from reality. Mind "in here"; matter "out there."

This is Cartesian dualism, mind and matter as two distinct kinds of substance that together compose the whole of nature. But how? What's the manner of their composition? Matter is solid geometrical stuff, spatially extended and nothing besides; mind is a mental substance, a thinking thing, period. We humans are compounds of the two—call them body and soul—conjoined by way of . . . well, actually, this is a conundrum. How can two kinds so fundamentally opposed fuse into one? Matter can bind to matter by physical contact, interpenetration, or intertwining, effecting change by pushes and pulls; and mind can associate with mind through intentionality—maybe; possibly; but, well, it's hard to say for sure. In any case, it's most definitely a mystery that a mind should fasten to a body such that if the body is pricked, the mind feels pain; or when the mind forms an intention, the body moves to enact it. The problem for Descartes is that, having split the world into distinct realms, he has no persuasive means of making nature whole again.

The problem for us is that, matter once severed from mind and left to its own devices, a device it became. Cold mechanism. Hence, the anti-teleological "mechanical philosophy." Lifeless and aimless, matter as mass, lumped clumps tossed around as corpuscles swirling in vortices or crashing atoms rebounding in the void, the machine grinding on by blind natural law. Suitable for study by physicists, no doubt; but inhospitable to liveliness or love; the natural world a mathematized blandness, spatial extension without appeal.

And on the other side of the divide, the "I" as a bottomless subjectivity, wrapped up within itself, thinking to itself, possibly of itself alone, there being nothing else. Who knows? Not the thinker, whose "knowledge" may be only one more errant thought, whose "I" itself may be but a fiction—as Nietzsche would later observe, it's an unwarranted assumption that there must be a doer behind the deed, an "I" behind the "think."

So the world of nature is quantitative matter, pale and lacking qualities. And the world of mind can think of matter but has no immediate contact with it. Our thoughts are become a figured veil between ourselves and the material world, and the result is "veil of ideas skepticism." If our access to the external world is mediated by ideas, we're confronted with the question whether our ideas reveal reality as it is. And there seems no way to know, for to compare ideas to the world beyond is a mental act effected by way of ideas, so behind the veil we find only more and more veils.

By infusing into western thought these seemingly insoluble perplexities, Descartes inadvertently prepared the ground for the rival ontologies of materialism and idealism, at least among those who could ignore the skepticism, or convince themselves they'd overcome it. So intractable a problem is the interaction of mind and matter that many have tried to resolve it by eliminating one or the other pole of the tension. Matter is actually mind; nothing beyond the mental exists, so there's nothing for our thoughts to affect or be affected by but other thoughts. Or our so-called "mind" is a fabrication of an overactive brain—all there really is is matter in motion, including whatever we regard as mental: our intending to move an arm, which causes our arm to move, is not a mental act mysteriously affecting matter; properly analyzed, it's just another phenomenon of mechanical activity.

So scientific materialism follows from Descartes' account of matter, and subjectivism or skepticism follows from his account of mind. Descartes himself didn't draw these inferences, but the unworkability of his dualism supplied the premises. The conclusions unfolded in time, and that time has since become known as Modernity.

18

Hume

What mischief has David Hume not wrought with his problem of induction? A problem for all empiricists. Empiricism: All knowledge comes only from experience—that's *all* knowledge, and *only* experience. Induction: To infer future events from past experience; to extrapolate general principles from particular observations.

The problem:

Acorns growing into roosters. It could happen, couldn't it? No doubt you doubt it. But on what grounds? You probably think yourself an empiricist. You probably think scientists are empiricists, too; most seem to think it of themselves. We'll see about that.

Imagine you're selling shrubs and trees, when into your establishment walks a strict empiricist. He demands assurances; one thousand acorns don't come cheap. Can you guarantee one thousand oak trees?

"Sorry," you demur. "I can't make such promises. So much depends on climate and the soil, when you plant the acorns and how you tend to them. It's unlikely, but it's always possible that none will grow at all. I expect that many will; but I can't predict the number, much less guarantee it."

But you've misunderstood the man. He's not worried about their growing; he understands the contingencies of sowing and reaping. What he wants to know is whether these acorns, if they grow, will grow into oak trees rather than, say, roosters. He's no chicken farmer, he grins.

"Roosters?! But they're acorns!" you protest, astonished. "They're not eggs! Acorns grow into oak trees, that's just what they do."

But he's not satisfied. How do you know that's what they do? How do you know that's what they'll do tomorrow—he hasn't even bought them yet, much less planted them and seen them sprout.

You're a mere manager of a nursery, not a philosopher. You know nothing of "essences" and "common natures," a material thing's participation in Form. And even if you did, your man wouldn't be persuaded: he's an empiricist, a nominalist, after all. And let's face it: you probably are too. You were born in the twentieth century, so it's unlikely you believe in anything beyond material individuals. There's no such thing as essences. So you try a different tack.

"Well, it's what they've always done, in the past I mean. So I guess I just assume they'll keep on doing it. Don't you?"

You don't sound confident, but I suppose that's understandable considering the circumstances. But, no, he makes no such assumption, and he marvels at your doing so. To him it seems unreasonable.

"Unreasonable?!" Now you're exasperated. "You're telling me it's irrational to assume that acorns will grow into oak trees?! Something I've witnessed many, many times in the past—you say it's unreasonable to expect the same thing to happen in the future under similar circumstances?! And you're worried about—what, roosters?!"

Yes, he's telling you just that, he says. Unless you can offer a guarantee that what's happened a thousand times must happen the one thousand and first time too.

First time . . . Hmm, for the first time now something sparks in your mind; you have a glimmer of what he's on about. "But I don't have proof," you think to yourself. "Mathematical or logical proof. I have only my expectations." And whence these expectations? From past experience, which to you makes perfect sense. Yes, of course it does: we learn from our experiences. Isn't that what they say? How else? Therefore, patiently you explain:

"Okay, I get it. I really do. So let me put it this way. In the past, whenever I've had many, many experiences of the same effect following the same cause—like something heavy falling to the ground when I drop it—it has always happened that in the future the same effect continued to follow the same cause. Things keep falling when I let them go, even to this day. And it's the same with acorns and oak trees: it has always happened precisely as I assure you it will happen this time! So there's your guarantee, if you want to call it that. Anyway, it's a reasonable expectation, I assure you." Pleased with the clarity of your exposition, you turn toward the back to retrieve the man's acorns, relieved to be done with so tedious a fool.

But not so fast. "So what you're telling me," he inquires, "is that, since in the past the future has resembled the past, in the future the future will resemble the past?"

"Yes!" you raise your voice now, triumphant. "Yes! That's it! That's how time works, right? Now you understand! So, if you'll just let me . . ."

Yes, he does understand, which he indicates with a lifting of his chin, and a frown. "But just to be clear," he says, "about time that is:

Let's assume I agree that *if* time works, as you put it, in such a way that the future resembles the past, then I also agree that oak trees will grow from your acorns. But suppose I'm uncertain whether time really works that way? What will you say to convince me?"

"Ha! Well, what *can* I say?! What can anyone say but that for as long as humans have been around it's always happened like that—the future's always resembled the past! Like I said, that's just how time works!"

"So I come to you in doubt whether oak trees will grow from your acorns. You assure me that they will because, you insist, the future will resemble the past. And when I doubt whether that is so, you assure me of it by observing that in the past the future has resembled the past. Is this what you're telling me?"

"Yes, exactly! That's it—just like that! So enough now with your roosters!"

"But I'm afraid it can't be just like that," he frowns again. "For listen: To infer from the fact that oak trees have grown from acorns in the past to the conclusion that oak trees will grow from acorns in the future, one must assume that the future will resemble the past. But why believe that? To infer from the fact that in the past the future has resembled the past to the conclusion that in the future the future will resemble the past, one must assume that the future will resemble the past—but that's the same assumption as before, and the very matter now at issue between us. You offer me y as a reason to believe x: very good, or so it seems. But then you offer me y as a reason to believe y. And now we're just running in circles. But of course that just won't do. It is, as I say, unreasonable."

And with that the man turns to leave, a spreading wake of silence trailing behind him. Stunned, you reach under the counter for your *open in case of emergency* store of bourbon. Twisting off the cap, you tilt the bottle over a plastic cup, and the "glug, glug, glug" as the whiskey pours sounds for all the world like "cluck, cluck, cluck."

A red feather circles lazily in a draft by the door.

. . .

How do you know that acorns, if they grow, will grow into oak trees, not roosters?

Because that's what's always happened.

And how do you know that what's always happened will always continue to happen?

Because that's what's always happened.

Ha! Well, yes. But again: How do you *know* that what's always happened will always continue to happen?

Well, so as not to repeat myself: I know that what's always happened will always continue to happen because the future always resembles the past.

And how do you know the future will always continue to resemble the past?

Because it always has.

You mean: Because that's what's always happened?

Yes, because that's what's always happened.

. . .

The problem of induction confounds philosophers and scientists to this day. So much so that scientists tend to ignore it. It makes them nervous, itchy, uncomfortable, because it discredits universal affirmations based solely on experience—which is to say it undermines the claims of science to be anything deeper than a practical or technological enterprise. A scientific "law" is an "always and everywhere" proposition, but no finite number of confirmations can justify a universal affirmation. Logically justify, you understand; psychology's another matter. As Hume was well aware, repeated experiences of conjunctions of specific causes with specific effects tend to condition us to expect the effect on the occasion of the cause. But that's a matter of habit, having nothing to do with necessary connections between the two events.[1]

Now you might think that practical application is good enough for you. Functionality is what we're after; no need to insist on truth. Fair enough; but consider this. If its advocates can't affirm the truth of science, they can't appeal to science to refute the truth of fields that contradict it (if and when they do), religion or metaphysics, for example. We may infer that x is false if it's contrary to y *only if* we *know* that y is true. If the truth of y is indeterminate, it can't serve as a standard against which to measure x or any other truth-claim.

You see the complications the denial of Being involves us in? It's not only morality and aesthetics that suffer, or philosophy and religion, but science too. Any endeavor with pretensions to objectivity must fail without the stable ground of Being to support it. The tide of Becoming will wash it away.

Oh, and one more thing: Hume doesn't believe in the self, either. When he turns his gaze around and looks inside, he finds no abiding unified subject of the many fleeting objects of experience, no "I" behind the "think." There's only the rushing river of Becoming; Being's been washed away.

---

[1] This failure of confirmation or verification explains why scientists are fond of touting "falsification," which was Karl Popper's solution—or rather his attempted evasion—of Hume's problem. Duhem and Quine showed the solution won't work, but still people go on appealing to it!

19

Kant

Kant scholars will forgive the contents of the present chapter. My aim isn't academic specificity or technical precision, especially regarding jargon. I hope only to communicate the consequences of Kant's thought for the matter at hand, in general terms broadly applied, and as his contemporaries and later generations understood it, not as the man understood himself or as specialists understand him today.

Let's begin by going all the way back to Democritus, an older contemporary of Socrates. From Protagoras' hometown of Abdera, Democritus was the founder of atomism (unless this honor goes to the shadowy Leucippus). He reasoned that matter is divisible into particles so very small they can't be seen by the human eye, but also that this division cannot proceed indefinitely. There must be some smallest bits that are indivisible, and these bits he called "uncuttables," *atomoi* (*atomos* in the singular). Like tiny material instantiations of Parmenides' One, these atoms are ungenerated, unchanging, and indestructible. They move in an infinite void, rebounding off each other or sticking together in clumps, composing thereby the objects of the natural world.

Democritus' atoms are characterized by size, shape, and position in space, but beyond that they have no attributes—no color, no scent, nor any other such quality or feature. Therefore, the properties we perceive of the objects made of atoms are not in the things themselves, but only in our experience of them. That is to say, for example, that since atoms have no color, neither do the things composed of them (and that's all the things there are). Color exists solely as a subjective experience in a mind interacting with the world through eyes. This holds for every other sensory experience too. "By convention sweet," wrote Democritus, "by convention bitter, by convention hot, by convention cold, by convention color, but by nature atoms and void."[1]

You may recognize this as a simplified version of our own contemporary view. Matter in the external world reflects light in waves of various frequencies, and this light interacting with a properly functioning human visual system generates an experience in that human's mind of color. But that's all color is—an appearance in subjective experience; it's not really "out there" in the things themselves.

So Democritus advocated a materialist view of nature, and in this he was surprisingly modern. Yes, there were modernists in the ancient world, as there are ancients around today (would that there were more!). In any case, Democritus' ideas were later taken up by Epicurus and his school, but they disappeared in the West with the fall of Rome. Pierre Gassendi, friend of Descartes, played a role in introducing atomism to early modern Europe, but earlier still Galileo

---

[1] The Greek words here translated by "convention" and "nature" are *nomos* and *physis*, as in the chapter above on Gorgias.

had argued for the main point at issue, which isn't atomism per se but the distinction between the natural world as characterized by objective spatial properties and all the other properties of things (color, odor, sound, taste, and feel) as strictly subjective. The former properties—those that are really in the things themselves—would become known as "primary qualities," the subjective properties as "secondary qualities."

So primary qualities are in the world itself, while secondary qualities are largely products of our minds. Those few teens who still learn things in school these days are taught this distinction in high school, though not with this terminology, and its metaphysical significance isn't often emphasized—reality as it is in itself is much different than it appears to be.

But what does all this have to do with Kant, you ask. I'll tell you: as the Moderns transferred to the mind properties formerly regarded as features of the external world, leaving only the spatio-temporal properties as mind-independently real, so Kant transferred these remaining properties to the human subjectivity as well. In his system even the "primary" qualities are secondary. Not just colors and odors and such, but three-dimensionality, temporal duration, substantiality, and causality too are imposed on our experience by the modes of operation of our perceptual and cognitive systems, or, more specifically, by the forms of human sensibility and the categories of our understanding.

With all the properties everyone thought were real extracted from the world and relocated in our minds, what remains in the world itself? One wonders. Kant does too, for he doesn't know. There's something there, he thinks (he calls it the "noumenon"), but it's inaccessible to us, an unidentifiable x. To know it as it is in itself, independently of our minds, we'd have to step outside our minds and then experience it—which of course we can't do. We can know it as it appears to us (as "phenomenon"), but only so; only as constituted by the categories of our experience.

Before we continue, it's important to note that Kant didn't say these things because he thought them trippy or wild and weird. He accepted that Hume had shown that empiricism undermines science, particularly by calling causality into question. We can never extract from experience alone knowledge of necessity or general principles; but Kant didn't doubt that we have such knowledge, as was evident to him from the success of Newtonian science. Therefore, he reasoned that the organization and operation of our minds introduce these necessities and principles into our experience. The world in itself is what it is (whatever that is); but the world we experience, from top to bottom, inside and out, is what our minds make it—and they make it to be a complex of causally connected substances described by Newton's laws.

You may have heard of George Berkeley, the Irish Bishop who advocated "subjective idealism," which is to say the view that only minds and their contents exist. Literally everything is mental. This is not Kant's position, not only because Kant believes in the "thing in itself" outside our minds (the noumenon), but also because his entire account of the operations of the intellect and the world's relation to it—known as "transcendental idealism"—is different, and much more elaborate. But, as I noted at the start of this chapter, I'm not here concerned to analyze these matters in granular detail. Scholars since Kant's own day have accused him of "Berkeleyism," and it's not my task to clear up the confusion. The main point stands either way: properties once held to be attributes of objects external to our minds—from their color and feel to their unity and spatio-temporal properties—are in fact products of our mind's interaction with the world. Literally every aspect of every item of our experience is generated by the structure and operations of our minds.

In Kant's system the subjective origin of the concepts and categories that structure the world of experience doesn't generate relativism. The configuration of the mind comes standard in all humans, and no options are available; all human minds operate the same from the same principles. So even though in a sense reality is "in our heads," we all inhabit the same reality because our heads are uniformly organized. This preserves for Kant a workable notion of objectivity.

But it wasn't long before various bold post-Kantian thinkers modified the master's system. For some, there's no noumenon behind the phenomena of experience, so the world in some sense is a production of the subjective "I." For others, the categories that organize experience are not in fact universal, so human experience isn't uniform. For some in this latter group, the categories change diachronically with changing historical epochs; for others, they differ even synchronically from culture to culture or, more radically still, from individual to individual. In all these ways and more, the objectivity inherent in Kant's original system gradually drains away.[2]

---

[2] I suppose this was inevitable the moment Kant determined that to solve the problems brought to his attention by Hume he should drive philosophy deeper into modern subjectivism—the concepts of our minds structure the world of our experience—rather than attempt a return to the classical or pre-modern objectivity of Being.

Arthur Schopenhauer, the philosopher who most captivated and influenced the young Nietzsche, was himself working in the Kantian tradition. As a student of philosophy, he concentrated on Plato and Kant; and in his major work, *The World as Will and Representation*, he introduces Platonic Forms into his account of the phenomenal side of the world (the representation), in contrast to the Will, which he took to be the noumenon, the true identity of Kant's supposedly unidentifiable x. A daring thinker with a keen interest in science, medicine in particular, his spin on Kant's ideas is distinctly naturalistic. Where Kant writes of the mind, for example, Schopenhauer writes of the brain.

Though Nietzsche eventually rudely repudiated Schopenhauer, many tendencies of his thought (in style as well as substance) track back to the older man's influence. Nietzsche too operates in the post-Kantian tradition, but in a manner shaped even more decisively than Schopenhauer by his scientific studies (especially in physics) and naturalistic inclinations. Particularly relevant here is the fact that Nietzsche thinks in the wake of Darwin, about whose work he had numerous reservations, but whose general account of evolution Nietzsche exploited in his theorizing about the origins, nature, and development of the "categories of reason," or the organization of our brain and nervous system, specifically our perceptual and cognitive apparatus, which structures our experience of the world. Our "knowledge" is for us what and as it is, not because our beliefs correspond to the "truth" but because they enable us to survive, or, better, to dominate.

20

Nietzsche

Platonism Inverted

Nietzsche the philology professor, when teaching Greek to his young students, used Plato's *Phaedo* as a text. His intention, he once remarked in a letter to a friend, was "to infect them with philosophy." But in the *Phaedo* there is a very particular brand of philosophy. It's not British empiricism, French materialism, or German idealism. I've called it "*Phaedo*-Platonism" to distinguish it even from Plato's other works. Not that it's different in fundamentals, but it is more anti-body than anything else in Plato's corpus. In the *Republic*, for instance, the philosopher-kings are selected from those who by nature are members of the warrior caste; so they must excel in fitness not only intellectually, but physically too.

In the *Phaedo* one encounters a perspective that Nietzsche would later condemn under the heading, "the ascetic ideal." At its most basic, asceticism is a privileging of the spirit or soul over the body, and really we should think of it even as a *repudiation* of the body for the (alleged) good of the soul. Broadly construed, it's a repudiation of the physical world in general undertaken to facilitate a reorientation from nature to the metaphysical or supernatural realm. According to the Platonic hierarchy of Being, since the One in every respect is superior to the Many, the eternal, unchanging, and immaterial is superior to the temporal, changing, and material; the soul is superior to the body; Forms superior to particulars; and the metaphysical superior to the physical, supernature to nature. Matter itself is the very principle of imperfection—it's the material element of a substance that constrains it from manifesting the Form in which it participates in all its unity and beauty. Matter is impurity manifest.

In the *Phaedo* we read that the body and its desires are to blame for all the conflict and other bad things in the world (66b–d). The body impedes our search for knowledge, subverts our commitment to virtue, and, if not properly disciplined, may even corporealize the soul, rendering it material and dense so that it can't fly away to its rightful home beyond the heavens but will instead reincarnate as an animal or linger on earth as an unhappy ghost haunting graveyards (80d–84b).

Philosophical purification (*katharsis*), a central theme of the *Phaedo*, is the separation of the soul from the body to the extent that it's possible while alive, true separation being literal death. Hence the famous expression that "philosophy is training for death" (64a, 80e–81a). So the philosophical ideal as expressed in the *Phaedo* is the *imitation of death*. It's no surprise, then, that a man like Nietzsche, who advocated a *philosophy of life*, would take aim at *Phaedo*-Platonism as at his principal adversary. All these thoughts and evaluations, and many more besides, are packed into his condemnation of the ascetic ideal.

Nietzsche read the *Phaedo*, as many do, as expressing Socrates' (or Plato's) aspiration after death to finally escape the cycle of rebirth and live forever without a body as a pure soul among the pure Forms. His doctrine of the eternal return—the idea that time runs in a circle infinitely repeating, so that every individual and event in the history of the universe recurs again and again in precisely the same configuration—this doctrine serves him as a counter-image to Plato's notion of escape.[1]

There is no soul apart from the body, so there's no opportunity for a man to escape his life. Socrates will be born again, as exactly the same man, in the same place, at the same time; he will live again the exact same life. He has already done so an infinite number of times, and he will never not be doing so. And since his consciousness will blink out at death, he'll have no experience of the passage of time among the living, no awareness of history's revolving round again to the hour of his birth, at which point he'll become again his conscious self. From his subjective point of view, then, the very moment of his death is the moment of his birth, unaware as he is of anything in between. So not only will Socrates live his life again, he won't experience any rest between the incarnations. Socrates is Socrates inescapably forever, always was and always will be, without respite or relief.

A gloomy counter-thought indeed to a man like Socrates, who regards his life as a prison sentence, his body as his cell. When the *Phaedo* opens, Socrates is released (*luein*) from the bond (*desmos*) on

---

[1] Paul Loeb is very good on this in *The Death of Nietzsche's Zarathustra* (Cambridge, 2012). See also his many essays on the eternal return. For an argument that the *Phaedo* does not teach permanent escape, see 'Notes on Plato and Nietzsche' in my *Diamythologômen* (S.Ph., 2019).

his leg that he might freely move his body about the room. As the dialogue proceeds, Plato employs precisely the same vocabulary to describe Socrates' death as his soul's release (*lusis*) from the bonds (*desmoi*) of his body. Socrates wants out of life like a felon sentenced to one hundred years craves liberation from his chains. But there will be no pardon; Asclepius, the god of healing, to whom he pledges sacrifice in his last words, will not purify him of the illness that is himself. Ever. This anyway is Nietzsche's counter-teaching to the *Phaedo*'s doctrine of escape. The eternal return. The eternal recurrence of the same.

Nietzsche's conception of his own philosophy as "Platonism inverted" is epitomized nicely in the eternal return in contrast to Platonic purification or escape. It's exemplified too in his insistence that "Being is an empty fiction."[2] Nietzsche's a Heraclitean thinker, a philosopher of Becoming. Properties that for Plato indicate ultimate reality—immateriality, changelessness, purity, simplicity, eternity—are for Nietzsche indications of nothingness, of the lie of Being masking the many unpleasant truths of Becoming—corporeality, change, power, conflict, death.

In Nietzsche's story of origins, the crack in the foundation of the universe—the lie of Being—derives, not from disobedience to God, but rather from misunderstanding and self-deception. Reason, Nietzsche writes—and by reason in this case he intends the interpretational tendencies generated by the organization of our cognitive system—reason directed inward, observing the interior workings of the individual, seems to itself to experience therein a

---

[2] *Twilight of the Idols*, "Reason in Philosophy" 2. I base the account of the origins of "the lie of Being" below on *Twilight of the Idols*, "Reason in Philosophy" 5. Do be aware though that this is but one of many such accounts Nietzsche explores in his works.

stable and enduring center and source of activity. This is (what we take to be) the "I," the ego, the self; and here is the origin of our notion of substance, our very conception of *being*. Each individual, regarding itself as an I-substance—a singular, unified, enduring subject at the base of a multitude of ever-changing properties, and the source of exertion, movement, and power—each of us, observing the world around, encounters "out there" many other swirling properties and movements that appear somehow to be associated with, and centered around, a singular source or ground; and, extrapolating from our experience of ourselves, we project our notion of the I-substance into the world at large and so conceive reality as populated by multitudes of stable, unified substances and their many changing attributes. In this way we construct the very idea of "thinghood." In short, *we think being into things*, behind things, *as* things, and thereby do we *create a world*.

So the human experience of reality as a field of substances and their properties—the one behind the many in all its guises—is a deceptive appearance manufactured by the functioning of our organism. And this organism is as it is, not because a deity designed it to track truth and seek goodness, but from the wholly natural forces of conflict and domination. Every individual, from the smallest particle to the mightiest beast, seeks to discharge its power into and against its environment, which includes of course many other individuals, each striving to exert its own influence on its surroundings; and those that most thoroughly establish their dominance over their rivals transmit to their progeny a nervous system whose structure and operation generate *this*, rather than *that*, sort of world.

The ontology engendered by these developments is eventually embedded in our linguistic practices, in their deepest strata even. The very grammar of the Indo-European languages, with their subjects and predicates, nouns and verbs, reflects our cognitively generated experience of substances and their attributes and activities, our experience, in a word, of Being. This phenomenon Nietzsche refers to as "the metaphysics of language": our misbegotten ontology is encoded in our language, so with every utterance—whether thought to ourselves or spoken to others—the lie of Being is promulgated again and again. When Nietzsche writes that he fears that we're not rid of God because we still believe in grammar—this entire assemblage of insights is in the background of this initially mystifying sentence. God is the ultimate being, and therefore the ultimate lie, because the very notion of *being* itself is a construct of the organization and operation of our perceptual, cognitive, and verbal-semantic systems.

21

Nietzsche
Metaphysical Nihilism

The quantity of material produced of late on Nietzsche and nihilism dwarfs the amount he published himself on the subject, which is next to nothing. This isn't to suggest that he had little interest in the matter. To the contrary, he associates nihilism with the problem of the meaning of the ascetic ideal, and in *On the Genealogy of Morals* he promised his readers a serious treatment in a forthcoming book ("Third Essay" 27). If at the core of the ascetic ideal is the overestimation of the value of truth, the very *will to truth* itself, then nihilism as the thought that "nothing is true" might seem to be a counter-ideal. And if it isn't that counter-ideal itself, it may well represent a way thereto, a path rising out of the muck of modern decadence to the heights of Zarathustran vigor and health.

When Nietzsche says that God is dead, he means, as he puts it in *The Gay Science*, that belief in the Christian God has become unbelievable (343). But he also means more than this. Platonism can survive the death of the Christian God, and maybe of all gods altogether. It cannot survive the denial of Being, however. So when Nietzsche writes of

"God" in a broad historical or metaphysical context, we should take it as a synonym for "Being." The death of God is the denial of Being in all its possible permutations.

Although Nietzsche published only a few remarks on nihilism, he wrote quite a lot about the subject in his notebooks. There's a longish late entry which, though mostly overlooked in favor of his few cryptic remarks on "active" and "passive" nihilism, exhibits a thoroughness of reflection and care in formulation that repays serious attention. It is, in short, a fine, concise description of the origins and nature of nihilism.

I divide my treatment of nihilism into two chapters: metaphysical and psychological; and I base this division on the note at issue—from Notebook 11, written between November 1887 and March 1888—in which Nietzsche tracks the onset of "nihilism as a psychological state" through three phases of development. The substance of each phase involves conclusions reached about metaphysical matters, and it's these we'll review in the present chapter.[1]

The first stage on the way to psychological nihilism is the realization that "Becoming aims at nothing." By this Nietzsche means that the history of the universe considered as a whole, the great cycle of return in which all things come to be, pass away, then come to be and pass away again, and again, eternally—this cycle is *just happening*, for no reason and with no future goal or end-state in view. There's no grand unifying narrative, no meaning, to events on a cosmic scale; nor is there any meaning on the scale of the individual. Many meanings have been

---

[1] *Writings from the Late Notebooks* 11[99] (Cambridge, 2003). As with the account of the "lie of Being" in the previous chapter, this presentation of the origin and nature of nihilism is based primarily on one of many accounts that Nietzsche explored in his notebooks.

proposed: the coming or the return of God; universal happiness; the moral world order; peace among the nations; even total annihilation by war or aliens or blind cosmic forces—any such final state would infuse the whole with meaning. We'd be heading somewhere, perhaps even intentionally (by the will of God, for example, or the designs of the administrators of our simulation), rather than just mindlessly moving, on and on and on, as apparently we are. Call all this the apprehension of *anti-teleology*.

This conclusion that Becoming is devoid of aim and meaning occasions fits of disappointment, embarrassment, and psychic exhaustion—oh, the waste of time and energy; the plans and hopes, anxiety and fear; the eager expectations, all in vain! Here we see one element of metaphysical nihilism generating nihilistic emotional and psychological states.

A second element of metaphysical nihilism is the loss of feeling of place, of *proper* place, of being somehow at home in the universe, precisely where one belongs as a part of an ordered whole. Think of the hierarchy of reality and value I've discussed throughout this text. Everything has its place, and there's an organizing principle running through the whole, binding the various constituents into a grand harmonious unity. Or consider the possibility that the many particulars are modes or manifestations of the one God; or, if not that, then creatures of the deity's design: either way we'd be oriented toward, and dependent on, a principle of perfection; we'd each be of value as a vital member of an infinitely valuable totality.

Now imagine thinking of oneself in these terms—and estimating one's value by these terms—and then one day, perhaps quite suddenly, being struck by the thought that, actually, none of this is so. There is no divine whole working through me; I'm not a child of God, nor an emanation or mode of his Being. I'm not a perfectly molded tile fitted snug right here where I belong in this cosmic jigsaw puzzle. No, I just happen to be here, now, and this "here" and this "now" aren't special; they have no orientation to any other "here" or "now" apart from my own subjective perspective. This second element of metaphysical nihilism we may call *cosmic homelessness*.

If the first two elements of metaphysical nihilism involve a loss of a certain type of faith in the nature and worth of this world, the third is the rejection of recourse to any other, "better" world. For one might be moved by weakness or fear (or both) to resist the threat of psychological nihilism by telling oneself that even though there's no meaning or order in *this* world, there's yet another world, *the true world*, where we can find a home, whether in this present life through the purification of a body-denying asceticism, or after death in another realm as reward for the proper exercise of intellect and virtue. But the honest man will not long fall for this ruse. He'll see through himself, into himself, to espy the machinations of a psyche in flight from pain, and he'll resist, admitting to himself that this "true world" is but the fabrication of a frightened mind. There's no other world than this, and this world is as barren of "truth" as it is of Being. Call this third element of metaphysical nihilism *the denial of any metaphysical realm or true world*.

Metaphysical nihilism, then, we may define as the "understanding that neither the concept of *'purpose'*, nor the concept of *'unity'*, nor the concept of *'truth'* may be used to interpret the total character of existence." Here we have a clear, accurate, and helpful account of one significant strain of Nietzsche's thinking about nihilism. It is, however, incomplete. As I've said, I've taken this material from just one of many notes—to my mind it's a particularly valuable note, but still it's only one.

In closing, then, I'll fill out the picture with a few quick insights from a short series of notes written while Nietzsche was traveling to the village where he penned the passage in the *Genealogy* promising more material to come on nihilism. Known today as "the Lenzer Heide note" (from the name of the town in which he wrote it), the first section details the elements of nihilism from which Christianity served as a temporary prophylactic. These include the feeling that humans are valueless, in part because of our ephemerality; the fear that evil and unredeemed suffering entail the world's imperfection and meaninglessness; and, finally, the thought that we're ignorant of absolute values and therefore have no idea what's important, or indeed whether anything is.

Later in these same notes Nietzsche includes as features of nihilism the rejection of the moral interpretation of reality (there's no hierarchy of value), the denial of God (there's no hierarchy of Being), the absence of objective values, and the meaninglessness of existence itself, which is infinitely compounded by the fact of the eternal return—"the most extreme form of nihilism" (*Late Notebooks* 5[71]).

It's evident that Nietzsche was still in the process of formulating thoughts about nihilism when he suffered his debilitating mental collapse. Who can say how he might have expressed himself had his reflections had time to mature? It's a great loss. But throughout his published and unpublished material there are recurring themes that at a minimum indicate the direction of his developing ideas. These include the death of God; the denial of Being; the meaninglessness of existence; the absence of objective values; the falsity of moral interpretations, whether of human actions or of nature and the world at large; and purposelessness in general, the "in vain" of all events, as is made explicit by the eternal recurrence of the same.

As these are insights into, or suspicions about, the nature of reality itself, I've labeled them "metaphysical." Although Nietzsche himself doesn't employ the phrase "metaphysical nihilism," it's useful because it facilitates our understanding of the important distinction between one's beliefs about reality (e.g., that life is meaningless) and one's psychological or emotional reaction to those beliefs (e.g., life isn't worth living). In the note we've been reviewing, Nietzsche provides the latter with the explicit label of "psychological" nihilism, so I've provided the former with a designation too: "metaphysical." The distinction between these two modes of nihilism is important, and should be made explicit, not only because, as a simple matter of classification, one's thoughts about reality are distinct from one's reaction to those thoughts but also, and more importantly, because Nietzsche means to emphasize that one may be a metaphysical nihilist without being a psychological nihilist, so the simple denomination "nihilist" won't suffice. One need not grow sullen and discouraged at the thought of the death of God. To the contrary, for the highest type of man the absence of God and Being is liberating, exhilarating, a source of cheerfulness. Unfortunately, these higher types are rare. For the great majority, if they ever do confront the reality of metaphysical nihilism, they'll inevitably succumb to psychological nihilism too.

22

Nietzsche

Psychological Nihilism

In the note under review on "nihilism as a psychological state," Nietzsche's focus is more on metaphysical than psychological nihilism, the causes more than the symptoms; but he does in passing provide indications of the psychological manifestations of the malady. We learn, for example, that the seeker of meaning becomes *disappointed* and *discouraged* at the vanity of all things; that he suffers from *agony, insecurity,* and *shame* at having deceived himself for so long about a supposed aim of universal history; his longing to admire and revere a supreme administrator is *frustrated*; and he *cannot endure the world* as he now understands it—a world with no metaphysical stratum, no divinities, no "beyond" or afterlife—but will not allow himself to deny it. In sum, he has arrived at *the feeling of valuelessness* of himself and reality at large.

These days, most everyone's heard of nihilism from its prominence in current culture, especially among young men. But many—including the young men themselves—lack a comprehensive understanding of its roots in intellectual history, the details of its anti-metaphysical assumptions, and even the specifics of its psychic manifestations. But those who suffer from it recognize that something feels amiss at a deep existential level. They're apathetic and unmotivated; they're lost; their pleasures and pains are wired into multifarious forms of virtual reality, some shiny and cartoonish, others dark and lurid; they're confused; they have no vision of a future life better than their present, no expectations of mature contentment or pride in adult accomplishments—indeed, they regard such talk as muddy managerial propaganda fed as slop to jobbers to keep them dragging into work to grow the bossman's wealth at their expense; they're lethargic; they're without hope; they're miserable.

We're familiar with the facts. But what can we do about the problem, as a people, as a culture, as individuals? Maybe nothing. But that may be just nihilism talking. Nietzsche has suggestions, including a sensible proposal in this note on psychological nihilism: if the cause of the condition is the realization that the categories of *purpose*, *unity*, and *truth* don't apply to the world, and as a consequence the world appears valueless, then maybe we should abandon our faith in these categories. Our belief that life and the world at large have value *only if* they can be interpreted in these terms is the precondition for distress at the realization that they can't be so interpreted. This leaves us with two options: (1) retain our faith in the categories and fall into nihilistic despair, or (2) dismiss the categories as the naive conceptual remnants of the immaturity of our species and stand before the world as it really is.

Once we understand that the *"categories of reason"* are the products of our own needs, aids to our survival and domination of the environment, subjective perspectives that we falsely project onto and into the objective world—once we understand all this we can "cancel our belief in" these categories. Once we have "*devaluated* these three categories," Nietzsche concludes, "demonstrating that they can't be applied to the universe *ceases to be a reason to devaluate the universe*" (*Late Notebooks* 11[99]).

As I say, this is a sensible solution. It's eminently reasonable; and it will work: *If you don't want there to be a God, it won't break your heart to learn there isn't one.* But it's demanding, and it's therefore also frightening, as discarding cherished illusions always is. Still, it's the only way to a genuine maturity, to adult autonomy and psychic health. Hard as it is to do, one must grow up.

It's an open question though whether Nietzsche's prescription will treat other conditions related to the death of God, cultural phenomena like decadence and the advent of the "Last Man." Cousins of nihilism, these two disorders exhibit symptoms with evident family resemblances; but each has its idiosyncrasies that are worth distinguishing and noting here.

Decadence isn't exclusively a consequence of the death of God, for it appears at least as early as the fifth century BC, among Socrates' peers. Though not reducible to, it at least involves something like an evolutionary decline of the species. The decadent animal organism is degenerate at its core, its dispositions or instincts having collapsed into anarchy, to the point that it positively chooses whatever is most harmful to it. The sequelae of this condition are many and deep, but in this context it may be helpful to mention just a few. Intoxication, for example: intoxication by alcohol or art, narcotics or moody mysticism, by sex or the longing for madness, excess pleasure or pain; intoxication even by the single-minded pursuit of knowledge, as in the man of science or mathematician plodding like machines; in short, every manifestation of immoderation employed as a means of escaping from oneself. And then there are the societal manifestations, the idolization of weakness and sickness, the celebration of revolt against nobility and every manifestation of authority, public pettiness, condemnation or mockery of all things great and historic. Even skepticism, pessimism, and nihilism may in some individuals be nothing more than intellectual expressions of physiological decay.

And this brings us to the "last men." As Nietzsche portrays the type in *Thus Spoke Zarathustra*, the last man seeks a life of comfort and ease, with no struggle or strife, a moderate and secure existence punctuated with a few small pleasures now and then to get him through his day. That's all he needs. Confronted with anyone striving for the future or personal accomplishment, the last man only blinks. The decadent will do what he can to tear all greatness down, driven wild by resentment and his own pathetic impotence; the last man on the other hand can't comprehend what all the fuss is about—he'd much rather nap in his easy chair with sportsball on the television. History has ended, after all. There's nothing to get hung about.

But to return to nihilism: Nietzsche begins the fifth book of *The Gay Science* with an entry headed, "The meaning of our cheerfulness." Here he describes the exuberance and joy, the sense of liberation experienced by the "free spirit" at the report that God is dead. And here it's relevant that Nietzsche later described himself as "the first perfect nihilist of Europe," adding that he had by then "lived through the whole of nihilism, to the end, leaving it behind, outside himself."[1] This personal history prepared him for the world-historic task of formulating a counter-movement to nihilism in and through a "revaluation of values," which is to say, a revision of our codes of Good and Evil drawn up in accordance with a new perspective made available by the death of God, the demise of Platonism, and the public exposure and condemnation of the lie of Being.

But despite Nietzsche's rejoicing at this civilizational cataclysm, he knows better than to take it lightly; and he admits that to others the event represents an enormous descending cloud of gloom. Unlike our contemporary clutch of shallow internet atheists, our enlightenment humanists and chipper "brights," Nietzsche understood that many chambers in the edifice of western culture rest on Christianity as on a foundation, our morality in particular. "The whole of European morality," he insists, "must collapse now that this faith has been undermined because it was built upon this faith, propped up by it, grown into it" (*Gay Science* 343). The death of God is a terrible occurrence, Nietzsche understands. We're bereft. The legacy of Greece and Rome still lingers, no doubt; but the calamity we face isn't only the demise of the Christian God, as I've already had occasion to mention. It's the denial of Being more generally, and the heritage of Being tracks back long before the birth of the Church; it runs through pagan Rome

---

[1] *Will to Power,* "Preface" 3 (= notebook 11[411]). To employ our terminology, I take Nietzsche here to refer to psychological nihilism—he has overcome nihilistic despair. He's still very much a metaphysical nihilist, though: God is still dead; being is still an empty fiction. Indeed, this variety of nihilism is a precondition of the revaluation of values of which he speaks.

and deep into the spiritual caves of Greece; probably even further still to the Indo-European warriors roaming the Caucasian steppe.

The grim, granite hierarchy of reality and value that towered over the West for millennia, the ancient pyramid whose ascending steps have measured for man all meaning and merit to date, the ladder of rank, the register of rule, the weights of worth so long and devoutly treasured as our divine inheritance—all this now collapses; it crashes around our heads and crumbles into dust at our feet. It's no laughing matter, not even if the glowering "teachers of the purpose of existence" are best overcome by laughter. It depends on who it is who's mocking them. Nietzsche was just one man, an exceptional individual; and anyway he's long dead. Many have been his disciples, or apes, but none so far his peer. Our "comedians of the ascetic ideal" today are fatuous and timid, small men, and more or less decadent (usually more).

And to be serious about Nietzsche himself for a moment: As rare a bird as he was, and despite his literary pretensions, he wasn't at all in his personal life a "free spirit"; nor was he particularly cheerful. He's revered today as an authentic figure who boldly "lived his philosophy," but what all this really comes down to is that he resigned his academic post (citing illness); he lived itinerantly (again, due to illness); he hiked (I don't say "climbed") mountains and walked in the woods; he brooded by lakes and wrote down his thoughts; and he retained more or less a consistent philosophical outlook for about fifteen years, despite being at odds with, and ignored by, popular opinion (that's *popular* opinion: other artists and intellectuals shared many of his insights and attitudes, though few expressed themselves as brilliantly).

Meeting Nietzsche in person, most of us would regard him as a prude, and ridiculously ingenuous. Unhappy too. His letters are full of melancholy, despair, and lamentations, frustration and bitterness, personal resentments, family squabbles, complaints about his physical state, and musings on suicide. The great man of Zarathustran boldness and laughter, the wild Dionysian flinging himself at fate, striding summits amid the clouds, and dancing near abysses—this was for the most part an authorial persona. Nietzsche's insanity gives it all a fine romantic shading—but, personally, I'd prefer from him a long work (or short; anything, really) written late in life, as we have from Plato in his *Laws*.

Nietzsche once wrote that "the Hebrew Jesus" died too young; and he made much of the fact that Schopenhauer's philosophy was a product of his youth. But Nietzsche himself died young too, twice. He went mad and ceased to write at forty-four; died at fifty-five. His intellectual and literary genius does much to mask the adolescent propensities of his thought, but they're present nonetheless. It's neither possible nor advisable to dismiss his ideas as the inflated cogitations of early manhood; but it's equally impossible reading him to mistake him for mature. He was dazzling, no doubt; but he wasn't yet ripe. He was still too much a child, of his long-dead father, of his mother who nursed him in his madness, of Schopenhauer, of Wagner, even of his own Zarathustra. Nor had he undergone the great metamorphosis into his second, more abundant and wiser, childhood—which comes, *if* it comes, only with age. Nietzsche was indisputably a philosopher of the highest rank; but he was no sage.

Did he ever even overcome psychological nihilism? For his sake, I hope so. But I'm not convinced he did.

23

Being and Becoming

From Platonism to nihilism: this is the history of the decline of Being, its dissolution into the flux of Becoming. Being is anything supposed to abide, from God to the smallest particle: it's Parmenides' Is-ing Thing, That-Which-Is; and it's Plato's Forms; it's Aristotle's substances and natures; it's Plotinus' One; it's Augustine's and Aquinas' God; it's even the materialists' matter, the "uncuttable" *atomos*; it's the soul, the self, the ego, the "I"; it's Truth, Goodness, and Beauty—Truth above all. Being is the Really Real, and Platonism is the conviction that there's such a thing in some form or other, and that all blessings in this life—and the next life, if there is one—hang on our knowing or communing with it.

The start of the Modern period, which we can date to roughly 1500, marks the moment Being began to collapse into Becoming, its foundations having been undermined by thinkers like Ockham, as we have seen. The Italian Renaissance shows early signs of slippage, especially among the Humanists of the fifteenth century, who attacked the scholastics and medievalism in general. The upheaval of the Reformation fragmented clerical authority, thereby making religious truth a matter of contention; the rise of the "new science" called traditional truths of nature into question, and in this connection the early modern theorists rejected Aristotle—known till then as *the philosopher*—especially his essentialism and teleology; the Galileo affair anticipated the later elaboration of biblical criticism, which would do much to alter the content of the faith; and the recovery of skepticism undermined confidence in man's ability to discover or comprehend truth of any sort.

Nominalism is the prime mover that sets all this in motion. There is no modern loss of Being without it, even though its original advocates were believers themselves (in God as Being if not in universals). The philosophers and scientists who initiated the scientific revolution believed in the Christian God, too; but many would rather peruse the book of nature than pray from the Good Book; many others declined to presume that we mortals have access to God's preferences and intentions, and so chose not to fret about them. Who after all can fathom the divine mind? Such attitudes soon evolved into Enlightenment Deism, the view that although the creator God exists, he (or, better, it) no longer intervenes in history, so the world and its inhabitants are on their own. The French *philosophes* of the eighteenth century were generally hostile to religion, and some were outright atheists; Hume's religious skepticism worried the faithful among his peers; and by the end of the century Kant convinced most thinking men that nothing at all can be known of God, the soul, or the afterlife. By the nineteenth century more and more the intellectuals—think here of Schopenhauer, Feuerbach, and Marx—were frank about their agnosticism or atheism. Then came Darwin's *Origin of Species*, published one month after Nietzsche turned fifteen, which seemed at the time to learned observers to have decisively destroyed the notion of teleology and, thereby, the most popular argument for God's existence.

All this history culminates in Nietzsche's declaration of 1882 that God is dead (*Gay Science* 108). And from the text of his announcement, it's clear that he has more in mind than just the Christian God; for the dead God casts a shadow whose blackness is an absorption of such "errors" as "the astral order"; "laws in nature"; "eternally enduring substances"; "matter"; "logical ideas and inferences"; "lines, planes, bodies, atoms"; "cause and effect." Notice that these errors cut across fields, from religion and metaphysics to physics, logic, and common sense. These erroneous notions are expressions of man's misguided deification of nature, and if we'd finally lay God (i.e., Being) to rest, and "naturalize" ourselves and the world, we must de-deify it all (*Gay Science*, 108–12).

And de-deify it we have. Indeed, this seems to have been the chief intellectual project of the twentieth century. From the Freudian counter-myth of God as a father-projection, through Existentialism's "existence precedes essence," to the Post-Modern deconstruction of meaning, identity, and logocentrism, and Critical Theory's critique of everything from bourgeois aesthetics to heteronormativity—wherever a lingering trace of Being is detected, it's targeted and attacked. There's nothing "post-" about any of this, of course. It's all just modernity churning out the conclusions of its initial premises; and the central assumption is that there are no forms, no essences, no natures. It's nominalism uncoiling: nominalism, empiricism, materialism, individualism, nihilism, absurdism, anarchism, perpetual revolution. Nothing is true; everything is permitted.

Read Nietzsche's discussion of that last expression in the "Third Essay" of his *Genealogy*. Read the entire essay, to my mind his greatest achievement. You'll find that his critique of the ascetic ideal—taking this formulation to encompass the belief in Being in all its manifestations—is far more thoughtful, and much deeper, than the aberrant reveries of his contemporary leftist admirers. Confronted with the notions propounded by the liberal nihilists and "post"-modernists who claim to think in his tradition, Nietzsche would be embarrassed: by the superficiality, the bitter baseness, by the resentment, ignobility, and the decadence of it all. It's enough to make a discriminating man long for the companionship of Plato. So wrong about metaphysics, but so dignified, so serious! And so right in so many ways about the social-political things! Just read his critique of the democratic regime and the democratic man in Book 8 of his *Republic*—the lack of order and necessity (*taxis* and *anangkê*) in the life of the man who lusts after "freedom" above all—and it's evident you're in the company of a noble spirit. Nietzsche once wrote to a friend that "perhaps this old Plato is my true great adversary," to which he added: "But how proud I am to have such an adversary!"

Strange to say, but as the river of Becoming flooded the fields of Being through the centuries, not all the land was washed away. Some tracts survived, underwater but undissolved. Esoteric Platonism—especially of the neo-Platonic variety—has flourished beneath the surface of the long, long history we've so sketchily surveyed here. It's the spine of Hermeticism, and it's near the center of Gnosticism; it seeps into late-ancient expressions of the mystery schools and the cosmogonies and cosmologies associated with them; it was influential in the formulation and development of Christian theology; it informs medieval mysticism, alchemy, and magic, and their elaboration in the Renaissance beside Kabbalistic metaphysics, Ficino's *prisci theologi*, and new strains of art and poetry; in the eighteenth century it's mixed up with anti-Enlightenment movements, from various secret societies to Romanticism; it informs New England Transcendentalism, Blavatsky's Theosophy, "cosmic consciousness," the Golden Dawn, Crowley's Magick, and Jung's mystical psychology. It's the beating heart of most every manifestation of perennialism and traditionalism.

And these days Being makes bold to appear even beyond the backrooms of occultism and esotericism. Despite the academics' refrain that everything's a "social construct," and their efforts to make "essentialism" a dirty word, Thomists and neo-Aristotelians argue a persuasive case that essences and teleology are inextricably embedded in the sciences, biology and physics in particular, and that the exclusion of these concepts from ethics is to blame for the untenable distinction between "is" and "ought" and various unsustainable anti-realisms, from emotivism to relativism.[1]

The centuries, the millennia stream past, yet Being abides. Year after year it carries on, as they say, burying its undertakers. Plato sheds a tear at Nietzsche's grave. Becoming will always be with us; but we mustn't exaggerate. You can tell yourself with Heraclitus, with Nietzsche, with Donald Hoffman or the simulation theorists that the oak tree outside your window isn't "real," is just a construct of your perceptual-cognitive apparatus, an icon on the desktop of your consciousness, or the product of a program running in the

---

[1] For example, David Oderberg's *Real Essentialism* (Routledge, 2008) and Edward Feser's *Aristotle's Revenge* (Editiones Scholasticae, 2019).

background of your mind to generate the tree and your mind too, and all the rest of the world including me and this book and these words. It's all just nerve impulses anyway, which are electrical-chemical reactions, which are transformations of energy, which are quantum fluctuations in a cosmic field that emerged from nothingness, at no time, nowhere, and for no reason. It's easy to think these things, especially for those of us raised on science-fiction, computer technology, and hallucinogenic drugs. "Nothing is real": we learned *that* when we smoked our first joint while listening to the Beatles.

But one day maybe you'll sit on your porch in the late afternoon sun, look at that oak tree in your front yard, and think: Don't be silly! That tree's there, and I'm not making it up or constructing it, much less making myself up; nor is anything constructing me inside its made-up self. That tree is what it is independently of me or anyone else; it has enduring, invariable characteristics; and it has these attributes regardless of who's looking at it or thinking about it with or through whatever "conceptual scheme." Of course it comes to be and passes away; of course it changes; and of course, as the Buddhists insist, it's embedded in networks of dependence of inestimable complexity. And, sure, you can plant a thousand trees around it and wonder whether it's an individual or a fraction of the forest, as you can wonder even now whether it's an independent "thing" or a collectivity of cells or molecules or atoms or subatomic particles or concentration points of energy, or power. A dream in the mind of a dreamt dreamer. Yes, all these thoughts are possible. And sometimes they're amusing. But are they plausible? Are they necessary? Are they serious?

It's an oak tree, not a rooster.

In Zen they say that, before coming to Zen, I thought mountains were mountains and waters were waters. Then, when I began to practice Zen, I thought mountains were not mountains and waters were not waters. But now that I've absorbed Zen, or been absorbed by it, I understand that mountains are really mountains and waters are really waters—but not at all as I had imagined them to be.

Personally, I like to imagine Plato and Nietzsche walking together and laughing about these things.

SUGGESTIONS FOR FURTHER READING

The following suggestions are meant primarily for the intelligent general reader, though in some cases the best available works are rather more narrowly academic.

For the Indo-Europeans, see Mallory and Adams' *The Oxford Introduction to Proto-Indo-European and the Proto-Indo-European World* (Oxford, 2006); Bruce Lincoln's *Death, War, and Sacrifice* (University of Chicago, 1991); and *To Fetch Some Golden Apples* (ed. Woodard; Kendall Hunt, 2006).

For the primary texts of the Pre-Socratics see Kirk and Raven's *The Presocratic Philosophers* (Cambridge, 1984) or the more recent collection edited by Daniel Graham, *The Texts of Early Greek Philosophy* (Cambridge, 2010). For secondary literature, I'm still partial to John Burnet's *Early Greek Philosophy*. Readers of this book will likely appreciate Nietzsche's *The Pre-Platonic Philosophers* (Illinois, 2006) and *Philosophy in the Tragic Age of the Greeks* (Gateway, 1996).

For an introduction to the sophists, see G.B. Kerferd's excellent *The Sophistic Movement* (Cambridge, 1981). See also *The Great Sophists in Periclean Athens* by Jacqueline De Romilly (Clarendon, 1998) and the Penguin Classics edition of *The Greek Sophists* (eds. Dillon and Gergel, 2003).

The best way to encounter Plato is to read the dialogues for yourself. But *do not use old translations*. The simplest solution is John Cooper's

Plato: Complete Works (Hackett, 1997). For Plato's *Republic*, however, I suggest Allan Bloom's translation (Basic Books, 1991); and for his *Laws* the translation by Thomas Pangle (Chicago, 1988) or the more recent one by C.D.C. Reeve (Hackett, 2022). The dialogues published individually by Hackett usually include introductions and notes not available in the *Complete Works*. The translations in the Focus Philosophical Library series are very good too. You also need to know something about ancient Greek history and culture, on which, see my suggestions in the Nietzsche section below.

See Charles Kahn's *Essays on Being* (Oxford, 2012) for information on the ancient Greek understanding of *to on*.

For Aristotle, Jonathan Barnes' two volume edition of the *Complete Works* (Princeton, 1984) is worth owning. Individual volumes published by Hackett are generally of high quality and include helpful notes and commentary. Hippocrates Apostle's translations are great, if you can find them. Robinson's *Aristotle in Outline* (Hackett, 1995) is a good little secondary text. Also very good is Carlo Natali's *Aristotle: His Life and School* (Princeton, 2013).

It's best to read Plotinus in either the abridged collection translated by Stephen MacKenna in *The Enneads* (Penguin, 1991) or the complete edition by multiple translators in Lloyd Gerson's *The Enneads* (Cambridge, 2019). For secondary literature I would highlight Pierre Hadot's *Plotinus, or The Simplicity of Vision* (Chicago, 1993) and John Rist's *Plotinus: The Road to Reality* (Cambridge, 1967).

The literature for a general audience on Sextus Empiricus and Pyrrhonism is sparse. For Sextus himself, Benson Mates' introduction and commentary to the *Outlines* in *The Skeptic Way* (Oxford, 1996) is very good; see also the Cambridge edition entitled *Outlines of*

Scepticism (eds. Annas and Barnes, 2000). For excellent, if somewhat technical, accounts of Pyrrhonism, see Richard Bett's *Pyrrho, his Antecedents, and his Legacy* (Oxford, 2003) and *How to Be a Pyrrhonist* (Cambridge, 2021). Charles Brittain's edition of Cicero's *On Academic Scepticism* (Hackett, 2006) is exceptional for those interested in the Academics.

Augustine's *Confessions* are essential reading; the translation by Henry Chadwick (Oxford, 2008) is good, as are Chadwick's *Augustine: A Very Short Introduction* (Oxford, 2001) and *Augustine of Hippo: A Life* (Oxford, 2010). The classic biography is Peter Brown's *Augustine of Hippo* (anniversary edition, University of California, 2013). Augustine's *Against the Academics* is very good for those interested in ancient Academic skepticism; see the translation by Michael Foley (Yale, 2019).

The literature on Thomas and Thomism is vast; I list here just a few of my favorites. Josef Pieper's *A Guide to Thomas Aquinas* (Ignatius, 1991); Joseph Owens' *An Elementary Christian Metaphysics* (Notre Dame, 1994); Norris Clarke's *The One and the Many* (Notre Dame, 2001); Edward Feser's *Aquinas* (Oneworld, 2009). And for a short, accessible, and thoroughly enjoyable experience of Thomas himself, you can't do better than Peter Kreeft's *A Shorter Summa* (Ignatius, 1993); though James Anderson's *An Introduction to the Metaphysics of St. Thomas Aquinas* (Regnery, 1997) is also a great selection of texts.

For late-medieval and early-modern thought, see Frederick Copleston's *A History of Philosophy*, volumes 2 and 3 (Image, 1993); David Lindberg's *The Beginnings of Western Science* (2nd edition, University of Chicago, 2008), which is also helpful for the study of the Ancients; M.J. Osler's *Divine Will and the Mechanical Philosophy*

(Cambridge, 1994) and *Reconfiguring the World* (Johns Hopkins, 2010); Edward Grant's *The Foundations of Modern Science in the Middle Ages* (Cambridge, 1996), and *A History of Natural Philosophy* (Cambridge, 2007). Convenient for Descartes is the Hackett edition of the *Discourse on Method* and *Meditations* (1999).

Hume's *An Enquiry Concerning Human Understanding* and *Dialogues Concerning Natural Religion* are accessible and of great interest. As for secondary literature, Don Garrett's *Hume* (Routledge, 2014) is very good. *Righting Epistemology* by Bredo Johnsen (Oxford, 2017) is wonderful for a history of skepticism focusing on Hume.

For Kant, who is difficult to read, maybe begin with the *Prolegomena to Any Future Metaphysics* (Hackett, 2001). For assistance, see Sebastian Gardner's *Guidebook to Kant and the Critique of Pure Reason* (Routledge, 1999); Henry Allison's *Kant's Transcendental Idealism* (Yale, 2004); and Paul Guyer's *Kant* (Routledge, 2014).

As with Plato, the best way to encounter Nietzsche is to read him for yourself. And, also as with Plato, *don't use old translations*. Walter Kaufmann's translations are readily available and quite serviceable (unless otherwise indicated, I quote them in this book); and the texts published by Cambridge University Press are good too. Even better than both are the more recent translations published by Stanford University in *The Complete Works of Friedrich Nietzsche*.

Apart from reading the man himself—and then reading him again, and again—the best way to get insight into Nietzsche's thinking is to know his biography, to learn something about Wagner, and to read Schopenhauer and the Ancients, the Greeks in particular.

For a brief account of Nietzsche's biography, see my *Zarathustra Stone* (S.Ph., 2016); for a fuller treatment, see Curtis Cate's *Friedrich*

Nietzsche (Overlook, 2005). See also *Selected Letters of Friedrich Nietzsche* (ed. Middleton; Hackett, 1996) and *Conversations with Nietzsche* (Gilman and Parent; Oxford, 1987).

For Wagner, Bryan Magee's *The Tristan Chord* (Picador, 2002) is a great place to start.

For Schopenhauer, at a minimum read volume one of *The World as Will and Representation* translated by Payne (Dover, 1966; volume one is the entire original work, the second volume consisting of later supplementary essays). Bryan Magee's *The Philosophy of Schopenhauer* (Clarendon, 1997) is most helpful.

For the Greeks, well, that's a vast subject; but certainly you must read Homer (use the Richmond Lattimore translations); the tragedians (Grene and Lattimore editions); the Greek Lyric poets, especially Pindar (William Race's two volumes; Harvard, 1997), and Theognis (see Gerber's *Greek Elegiac Poetry*; Harvard, 1999); Herodotus (*The Landmark Herodotus*, Vintage, 2009); Thucydides (*The Landmark Thucydides* is most helpful [Free Press, 1996], but Steven Lattimore's translation [Hackett, 1998] is more accurate); Xenophon (it's all valuable, but most relevant is the *Memorabilia*, the Loeb edition of which is useful, with a revised translation by Henderson: Harvard, 2013); and, of course, Plato.

As for secondary literature, there is much to avoid, the French postmodernist readings of Nietzsche principal among them. There is much that is good too, of course; so much that I limit myself to listing a few of my personal favorites. Bruce Detwiler's *Nietzsche and the Politics of Aristocratic Radicalism* (University of Chicago, 1990); Robin Small's *Nietzsche in Context* (Ashgate, 2001); John Richardson's *Nietzsche's System* (Oxford, 2002); Brian Leiter's

Nietzsche on Morality (Routledge, 2002) and *Moral Psychology with Nietzsche* (Oxford, 2021); Michael Steven Green's *Nietzsche and the Transcendental Tradition* (University of Illinois, 2002); *Nietzsche and Antiquity* (ed. Paul Bishop; Camden House, 2004); *Nietzsche's Anthropic Circle* by George Stack (Rochester, 2005); Thomas Brobjer's *Nietzsche's Philosophical Context* (Illinois, 2008); Paul Loeb's *The Death of Nietzsche's Zarathustra* (Cambridge, 2012); *Nietzsche and the Philosophers* (ed. Mark Conard; Routledge, 2016); Hugo Drochon's *Nietzsche's Great Politics* (Princeton, 2016); and Laurence Lampert's *What a Philosopher Is* (University of Chicago, 2017).